WHAT BLACK WOMEN DON'T KNOW ABOUT BLACK MEN (BUT NEED TO KNOW)

Kareem Rice

Much happiness and success in life and in love and in college

Kareem Rice

K O Publishing Co.
P.O. Box 34456 Philadelphia,
PA 19104

www.kopublishingcompany.com

Manufactured in the United States of America

This book is dedicated to all women.

CONTENTS

If you remember and believe that each new day you are blessed to see is a chance for a new beginning, then nothing can stop you from finding love, happiness, and peace of mind.

Preface

Black women, are you tired of all the games that black men play? Black women, are you tired of all the lies that black men tell? Black women, are you tired of all the headaches, the heartaches?

If you are, this book will help you recognize the men you are meeting in these crazy times before you let them into your lives and homes or around your children. Such awareness can help you escape from present headaches and avoid future heartaches. It may even go a long way to ensuring your happiness, safety, and peace of mind.

I wrote this book to try and spare black women like my mother, aunts, sister, daughter, cousins, friends, and co-workers from pain and even death at the hands of black men who only care about themselves, who use, lie, cheat, control, and abuse until it's too late and their women have been hurt.

As a black man, I know that there are a lot of sick, dangerous, and evil black men in the world. This book gives you the tools—the knowledge, the facts, and the information—to tell a good black man from a black man who's a player, a user, an abuser, a cheater, a control freak, or a criminal. With knowledge there is protection and power over your life.

Black women, there are black men who can destroy your life if you are not careful. In these crazy, unpredictable times you can't trust a stranger just because he looks good, has a nice smile, a good job or his own business, and drives a snazzy car. These things don't stop him from being a user or an abuser.

I know. I was once a player, a liar, a user and a cheater. But I have never put my hands on a woman and I never will. That's a lesson I learned from my mother and I've loved her for it. When I was around ten years old, she sat me down and said if she ever heard about me hitting a girl, she would whip my ass herself. I was always, she instructed, to have respect for all women.

I have broken hearts in my time, with my lying and cheating ways, but I have never for the life of me understood how a man could want to hurt, even kill, the woman he says he loves. Yet I have watched black men I have known most of my life kill the women they say they love. They never did love these women; you can never physically hurt someone that you truly love. That's not love, and black women need to be careful, alert to the warning signs that a black man may be dangerous to them or to their families.

When I started writing this book, I focused on what black men like or don't like, where black women could meet black men, how they could understand black men better. I talked to black men everywhere—men I played sports with or worked with, that I hung out with at night clubs and the recording studio that I managed or I met on the streets. What, I wanted to know, did they look for in black women? How did they treat the black women in their lives? What did they want out of a relationship with a black woman?

After talking to black men from different cities and states, with different life styles, I realized that the majority of black men were on a different page when it came to marriage or committed relationships and their casual involvements. While a minority of black men asked questions and listened, the majority focused their exchanges on how not to get caught cheating or lying to a wife, fiancée, or girlfriend. The consensus was that what the woman didn't know wouldn't hurt her. When one of them got caught cheating or lying, the others didn't offer consolation—"I feel for you" or "I understand what you're going through." They criticized: You should have done this or that; to get away with seeing another woman, you've got to do this or that.

There are a lot of good loving and honest black men out there, but there are also many players, users, and abusers. In most metropolitan cities black women outnumber black men almost ten to one and the statistics can be even higher in certain areas. With black men making up 56 percent of the incarcerated population in the United Sates, with 64 percent unemployed, 24 percent homosexual, and 42 percent dependent on drugs, alcohol, or both, only a small percentage remains. There are few good honest black men to choose from nowadays.

If I don't know about a subject and haven't researched it, I don't write about it. From my interviews with black men and black women as well as my personal experiences, I have no doubt that black men play more games than women when it comes to relationships. Many black men enter marriage or a relationship with thoughts of cheating already on their minds. Some start a new relationship when they're already involved with another woman. That's another reason for black women to be careful about the men they let into their lives.

Most black women begin their relationships with love and trust toward their partner. But then he starts messing up until they cannot take any more of his cheating and lying ways. Few black men give black women credit for being wise to the games they play until they're caught. Yet when black women start running around playing the same games, they get upset.

This book is for black women and women who are in relationships with or married to black men or are interested in dating black men. It is not about white men, Hispanic men, or Asian men.

I write from personal experience playing the games and from growing up around players. I have talked to and listened to black women who have been played, hurt, abused, and used by black men they loved and thought loved them. I have talked to and listened to black women who play the game with black men and love playing it.

American society is more open-minded about different kinds of marriages than ever before in its history. So my book is also for black women who are in relationships with or married to white, Hispanic, or Asian men—but only if those men have black male friends. Why? It's widely recognized that black men are great at influencing other cultures when we come into contact with them. You see the phenomenon every day in fashion styles, music, food, and sports.

This book applies to the games of tomorrow as well as those of today. Most players, cheaters, and abusers don't change their ways;

they just learn from their mistakes and get back to playing. Because there are patterns in the ways the games are played, you can learn to read the danger signs. In other situations, you might need to take steps to save your marriage or relationship before it gets to the point where he wants to cheat.

A lot of women out there—not just black women—have been played, used, or abused by black men and kept quiet. They are too embarrassed or too hurt to talk about the experience or to warn others. But that knowledge is a weapon. If you have knowledge of something that can harm, hurt, or even kill you or someone you love, you're better prepared to handle the situation when you're faced with it. With no knowledge, you are all too vulnerable.

This book will help you understand the games black men play—how some care about nothing but themselves; about the engagement games when they have no intention of ever marrying; about black men who live two parallel lives or have sex with their partner's female relatives or friends; who pay for sex because they can't get enough at home; about black men who will always be users, abusers, and cheaters no matter how good their women are to them. I wrote this book to increase awareness of the games being played by black men so that black women don't become victims or statistics. There are a lot of good black men out in the world. It's just harder to find them, and they are way outnumbered by black women. As a result, many black women let black men get away with having other women or other families in their lives. They would rather share a black man than not have a man at all. And, too, a black woman often makes it easy for a black man to cheat. She simply goes along with anything he does or tells her.

This book is for black women who don't want to be the other woman, the side chick, bottom chick, or mistress. I went from writing a book to help black women meet and understand black men better to writing about how they can recognize the players out there before they get themselves deeply involved and risk harm. If you don't want to know the truth about black men, then stop reading and give the book to another black woman who does.

If my book prevents only one woman from being harmed, hurt or even killed, then it has been worth all the time, research and effort. I hope and pray that the book helps you—in a small or a big way—to find happiness, love, and peace of mind and heart that we all seek in life.

Life is too short for games and to withhold valuable information about the games black men play is, I believe, a sin. This book holds nothing back and pulls no punches; it keeps nothing from you. You need to know the truth because it can be so dangerous to be involved or get involved with the wrong black man.

The following chapters chronicle all the games black men play and alert you to the warning signs so you won't be taken in by those games. The advice ranges broadly: How to tell whether or not your husband/fiancé/boyfriend is a player or if he has another family on the side you don't know about. You'll get the lowdown on strip clubs, gentlemen's clubs, and bachelor parties and what really goes on there. You'll discover ways to find out if that woman is actually a relative or an ex and how to test whether that fiancé is serious about getting married or just playing you.

Throughout, the advice draws on the actual experiences of black women—what can happen, say, when you let a female relative move in or what you can do if you suspect your husband/fiancé/boyfriend might be seeing an ex on the sly. You'll find tips on how to handle a Mama's boy and a wealth of information on HIV/AIDs, which is affecting black women at alarming rates.

In short, you'll discover wide-ranging advice, based on the stories of hundreds of real men and women as well as my own experience as a player. These accounts not only reveal the strategies and techniques players and hustlers employ. They also point to warning signs, signs that will help you avoid or get out of a relationship with a player or hustler and into a healthy, rewarding one with a good black guy who won't play games with your life and your heart.

Chapter 1

In the Beginning

Everything isn't always as it seems. If he's
too good to believe, or too good to be true,
then you need to check what he tells you to
see if he's who he says he is
before you trust him
with your heart, mind, and body.

Black men know that there are black women out there who want to be in honest loving relationships and one day even get married and have children. Black men also know that there are black women who love playing the same games and tell the same lies they do. As a result, many black men only show so much of their true selves. They wait until they know where the woman is coming from. These black men are going to play it safe and guard their emotions until they can be sure that she is really into him for who he is, and not for what he has or what he can do for her.

Then you have the other kind of black man who is out to use and abuse, will lie and cheat and play any woman he can get his hands on until he is tired of the game or she is all used up, burnt out physically, mentally, emotionally, and financially.

A lot of black men who are players start off a relationship with a great act, putting on a sincere front. They wear a mask until they feel in control of you and the relationship. In this chapter, I will show you warning signs to help you spot a player and offer tips on what to look for in a good black man.

Warning Signs That He Might Be a Player

1. After knowing him for a few weeks or months, he still has not invited you over to where he lives.
2. After knowing him for a few weeks or months, you still don't know where he lives. But he knows where you live and has even been over to your place a few times.
3. When making plans—to go out for dinner or to the movies, say—he always wants to meet you at your place or where you are going.

If he's doing any of these things, then you must take a moment to check what other things he might be up to and keeping from you. Always give him the benefit of the doubt, but not after his behavior corroborates your suspicions. Not all the observations made in this book apply to every black man. Many are honest and sincere about their marriages and their relationships. The trick is to identify the good ones.

Things a Black Man Does Who Is Sincere About Getting to Know You

1. He calls you at least once a day to see how you are doing and to let you know that you have been on his mind. He'll tell you to have a nice day at work or to be careful driving home.
2. He calls to tell you that you were the first thing he thought about when he woke up and that he'll be thinking of you all day.
3. He calls you to make plans to meet for lunch or dinner—his treat.

4. He calls you after you get off work to see how your day was. Depending on how far the relationship has progressed, he will ask whether he should bring dinner over to your place or cook at his place.
5. He calls to see if you need anything done or need a ride home from work.
6. You know where he lives; he's invited you over to his place at least once.
7. He's given you his cell phone number and his home phone number.
8. He'll ask you to meet him at his place before going out for the evening.
9. He talks to you about his family and his child/children without you having to ask him about them.
10. He's told you where he works and what he does for a living. If he gives you his work or business number, he's really into getting to know you and sincere about building a relationship with you.

In the beginning of any relationship with a black man, you have to test where him mind and heart are when it comes to you. Trust your gut feelings. Often you will find that your initial reactions were spot on. But your gut feelings will not always be right. That's why you need to have the facts—the real reason, say, why he hasn't invited you over to his place—before you get into any confrontation.

Reasons Why He Has Not Invited You Over

1. He might be playing it safe. There are crazy black women out there, not just crazy black men.
2. He might be protecting his privacy until he decides if he's really interested.
3. He might be afraid that if you know where he lives, you will be able to retaliate if you break up—smash up his vehicle or

cause a scene. He doesn't need the hassle; it was just sex for him.

4. He might want to avoid any possibility of drama in case things don't work out. He doesn't care that you might need closure; he just wants it to be over so he can get on with his life and seeing other women.
5. He might be a player and have another woman coming over or living there. It's too risky. You might run into her.
6. He might live with his wife/fiancée/girlfriend and not want you to know.

You need to find out what's behind his hesitation. If, after two or three months of seeing each other, you still don't know where he lives or haven't been invited over to his place, it's time to bring matters to a head. He might simply be embarrassed—he still lives with his mother, his place is a mess, or he's worried about his roommates' reactions. If, as you suspect, his sincerity is doubtful, move on. Stop wasting your time. Otherwise you will probably be setting yourself up for headaches and heartaches.

Be smart once the warning signs are clear. Once you know the truth, what's really going on with him, you can learn from the experience and move on with your life. Unless you do learn from the experience, however painful, the next man who crosses your path will most likely feel that pain and he might not be understanding or patient enough to stick around.

A lot of black men will say and tell a woman just what she wants to hear to get in between her legs and in her pockets. When he's taken all he wants or she's all used up, he's gone about his business and onto his next victim. That's why you must check who you let into your life, into your heart, and into your home at the very beginning of a relationship. Trust no man one hundred percent until he earns one hundred percent of your trust or close to it.

Warning Signs That He Might Be Lying to You

1. He idly touches or strokes his throat. When a man feels threatened or worried about being caught in a lie, he tends to touch his neck area. He'll fix his shirt or mess with his necktie.
2. He'll rub his eyes as if there's something in them. He is consciously or subconsciously trying to avoid direct eye contact with you. If he wears eyeglasses, he'll take them off and pretend they need cleaning.
3. His voice level changes or he'll clear his throat as if he needs something to drink.
4. His facial expression changes when you ask him a question. His nose will crinkle up as if there's a bad smell around.
5. He'll smile too much or he'll get abnormally serious when you question him about something or someone.

Research and personal experience have taught me that black women tend to trust black men one hundred percent straight off in their relationship. Then he messes up big time and is caught lying or cheating. The cycle repeats and the lies and deceit pile up until there is no trust or love left. But by then it's too late. The damage has already been done. That's why I advise black women not to give their trust, body, and heart blindly. Make him earn that love and trust.

Make Him Earn Your Love and Trust

When you first meet a man you are attracted to and you think is interested in getting to know you, be nice, but treat him as you would treat a job applicant if you were the boss. Have him tell you about himself. How old is he? Does he have any children? Is he married or separated from his wife? Does he have any children by her? How many children? What are their ages? What are his thoughts about relationships between men and women? Does he believe in open relationships? (If he says yes, then he's into seeing other women while in a relationship with you,) Does he believe in monogamy? (If he says yes, then he believes or is pretending to believe in fidelity.)

He may not be telling you the truth. Black men play a lot of games. Everything isn't always as it seems. You need to ask questions like these because his answers will give you some insights into his character as well as information about his past, his present, and maybe his future plans. If you don't ask any of these questions at the beginning of a relationship, when things that you didn't know about start coming up—other women, children, child support, and alimony—he's going to defend himself and say that you never asked. He's not going to admit that if he had been sincere about you and the relationship, he would have told you. Actions speak louder than words. Words are just words until they're put into action.

The beginning of a relationship is like a job interview and he's the applicant; you're the boss. You want to decide whether he's worth dating or getting involved with. I've come to realize through my many years of research and personal experience that black women don't ask the important questions when they meet black men for the first time. These questions can save a lot of headache and heartache, but they don't get asked.

Often black women don't feel they have the right to ask a man they've just met personal questions. You absolutely do have the right if he wants to be a part of your life. Ask whatever questions that you feel you need answered and tell you what you want to know about him. If it's too personal, he'll tell you, believe me. If he doesn't answer the questions you feel are important, then you need to take a mental note and file it in your head for later or end the interview then. Don't waste your precious time with the "I can't answer that now" or "Wait until we get to know each other better" games. Life is too short. Why waste it playing games with a grown man who should know better?

Women have told me endless stories about how *not* asking questions tripped them up later. One woman dated a man for six months before she found out that he was married. Why? She never asked him; she just assumed he wasn't since she never saw him with a wedding ring. Had she discovered he was married before they got emotionally and physically involved, she would have saved herself a pile of trouble. Another woman found out after almost a year of dating a man that he liked to get high on drugs. She never asked him or his friends.

Black women must guard and protect their trust, body, and heart. Don't give them to a man easily, simply because he talks a good game, has a great smile, a nice body, or drives a fancy car. You have only one life to live so why take a chance on trusting someone who might not care about putting your life or maybe a family member's life on the line? In these crazy times you have to be very careful about the people you let into your life. The owner or manager of a company would never think of entrusting the keys to the business or the security code to the alarm system to a new employee. So why would you give a man you have only known a few weeks the keys to your vehicle, to your home, or your heart and access to your body whenever he likes?

Most new employees undergo a probationary period lasting six months to a year because the company managers don't really know them, no matter what their applications or resumes say or how great the interview went. The new recruits need to be around for a while before a manager can get a read on their character and trustworthiness. If the newcomers don't measure up or mess up, the company won't hesitate to let them go. Your life is more important than any job or career. When you first meet a man put him on probation—while you see where the relationship might go. He needs to earn your trust.

Earning Trust Points

There are many ways for a man to earn percentage points on your trust meter. Something he has told you about himself turns out to be true or something he does makes you smile and feel great on the inside. A few examples:

1. He calls when he says he's going to call the majority of the time.
2. He usually meets you or picks you up on time.
3. The information he has given you about his past or his children turns out to be accurate.
4. He's in the process of getting a divorce, just like he said.
5. He is sincerely concerned about how you are doing and feeling during the day or the week.
6. He calls you in the middle of a busy day to check up on you and to see if you need anything.
7. He remembers dates and events that are important to you.

On the other hand, he loses points on the trust meter if something he's said about himself proves to be a lie or if he consistently is late meeting you, seldom calls, and forgets important dates.

A black woman once told me that in every relationship she gave one hundred percent of her trust, heart, and body. All her relationships ended in heartbreak. Why? She trusted the men who came into her life one hundred percent when she knew hardly anything about them. So often burned, she vowed never again to trust a black man, fully convinced that no black man was to be trusted, that black men cared about nothing but themselves. I told her that wasn't true: there are a lot of good black men out there who are honest, loving, supportive, loyal, kind and caring toward black women. The trick is to be able to tell the difference, to separate the good ones from the players.

Chapter 2

The Cell Phone Games

Communication is one of the keys
to a successful relationship and marriage.
Without it, you have nothing but an empty shell of a life.
In all relationships two people become one when they share and
express what's on their minds and in their hearts.
With communication, love and trust grow stronger.

The cell phone game is a major tool in a player's arsenal because communication is such a key factor in relationships. If you can't get in touch with your partner when you want or need to, something is very wrong with your relationship.

Patterns in your communication give off strong signals as to whether or not your partner is a player. You can usually get in touch with a black man who's not a player—unless he's at work. Many jobs don't allow cell phone use at work or are in areas where he can't receive a signal.

Just because you can't get in touch with him when you call doesn't mean he's a player; it definitely means you have a communication problem that you need to address before there's no husband, fiancé, or boyfriend to call in the future. But the inability to connect via cell on a regular basis is a worry because it is a major characteristic of a player. Before you jump to conclusions, however, you need to get the facts, proof that he's avoiding your calls or hiding his.

A great many excuses are used to explain why a call goes unanswered. Some may be perfectly legitimate so don't jump the gun and automatically assume your husband, fiancé, or boyfriend is a player. Your suspicions need to be substantiated before you confront him.

Warning Signs That He Might Be a Player

Players employ a whole range of excuses to justify their unavailability. These excuses become warning signs when you hear them regularly and can seldom get in touch. Pay particular attention if he routinely calls you back ten minutes to half an hour later rather than picking up right away. Typical excuses include:

1. I didn't hear my cell ringing when you called.
2. I cut my cell off because my battery was low and I left the charger at home.
3. I didn't realize my cell phone was turned off. I must have turned it off by mistake.
4. My cell phone went dead because the battery wasn't charged before I left.
5. I had the music up loud while I was driving and didn't hear my cell phone ringing.
6. There was so much music and noise—at the night club, sports bar, football game, or basketball game—that I didn't hear my cell phone ringing.
7. I left my cell at home by mistake.
8. I left my cell in my car or truck by mistake.
9. I had my cell on vibrate and left it in my coat or jacket pocket.
10. I lent my cell to my friend [hommie, brother, cousin], and didn't notice that I had missed a call from you when he gave it back.

11. I dropped my cell and it's been acting up ever since. Sometimes it rings and sometimes it doesn't.
12. I left my cell on the charger in my car or truck.

Batteries do run low; cell phones get left behind; sometimes it's hard to hear the ring tones or there's no signal. These things happen—but not all the time. Being able to communicate with you partner is so very important to the relationship and cell phones are a major means of communicating these days. But they are not the only means.

Another warning sign to be on the lookout for is a reluctance to give you all his numbers. You've been seeing each other for a while, but you only have his cell phone number—not his home or work numbers—and you've been having sex with him. This is a really ugly sign for any future relationship; most likely there won't be one. You're just lying to yourself if you believe that there will be if he doesn't respect you enough to give you his home number.

What's really crazy is how he probably has your cell phone number, home number, work number, e-mail address, and maybe even your mother's home phone number because you're there a lot and you want him to be able to get in touch with you whenever he needs or wants to. If, after being involved with you sexually for weeks, if not months, a man won't give you his home number, you need to stop, look, and listen to what's really going on in your so-called relationship. That unwillingness to share lines of communications means he's not serious about the relationship. You're just a jump off, a booty call.

The Multiple Cell Phone Problem

Black women need the 411, the low down, the what's what on why some black men have pagers or extra cell phones or burner phones. They keep these extra cells private for a reason and that reason usually isn't good news for any relationship.

Why He Might Have an Extra Cell

1. He's hustling and can't or doesn't want to give the people he's dealing with his personal cell phone number just in case something goes wrong with any of his illegal dealings.
2. He has another woman or women he's seeing and needs a spare cell because he uses his personal cell for your communications.
3. He has a prepaid phone because it is impossible to track the phone calls he makes or receives on it.
4. He has an extra cell phone because he's involved in business he's not ready or willing to tell you about.

Warning Signs That He Might Have an Extra Cell

1. He goes to another area of the house or apartment to be alone when you're at home with him.
2. All of a sudden he has to get something or needs to look for something in the basement, garage, or attic.
3. He has to go outside to his car or truck a lot.
4. He has to run out for something—food, gas, etc.—when he said he was in for the night.
5. He disappears to another part of the house or apartment for five or ten minutes.
6. He's alone in the room and has the T.V. or stereo turned up loud. When you ask why, he has no real explanation other than he felt like it. The noise level ensures you can't hear him talking on his extra cell phone. You just saw his personal cell phone on the table in the other room so it never crosses your mind that he's talking to someone on another.

If these things happen a lot, then there's a great possibility that your partner has a cell phone that you know nothing about.

Most of the time, when your husband, fiancé, or boyfriend has a cell you don't know about, he will check his messages and missed calls by calling his other cell phone from his personal cell phone right in front of you without you realizing what's going on. He will never use the home phone to check his messages and missed calls because you might pick up the phone while he's checking. He might have to go to another part of the house or apartment or run out all of a sudden so that he can call back the people he's hustling or involved with in his illegal dealings.

What He Might Tell the Other Woman When He Calls Her Back

The excuses he might use when he calls the other woman back are ominously familiar. You've probably heard variations yourself.

1. I was busy working and couldn't answer my cell phone when you called.
2. I was busy fixing my car or truck [or someone else's car or truck], and I didn't hear my cell phone ringing.
3. I was at the gym working out [or playing basketball, etc.] and I didn't have my cell with me when you called.
4. My battery is low and I turned my cell off until I get a chance to recharge it.
5. I couldn't talk because my prepaid minutes ran out, and I had to buy some more before I could call you back.
6. I was in a meeting, or talking business, and I couldn't answer my cell phone when you called.
7. I don't know why, but my cell phone didn't ring when you called. Maybe I wasn't getting a good signal where I was.
8. I was at the hospital and had to turn my cell phone off. I just got out of the hospital so that's why I'm calling you back just now.

9. I had to work overtime, and I didn't know until the last minute so I couldn't answer my cell phone until now.

Pay attention if the man you're seeing or are in a relationship with is calling you back with some of these excuses. When he doesn't answer his cell phone when you call him, then maybe, just maybe, you might be the other woman and not even know it.

Warning Signs that You Might be the Other Woman

1. He hardly ever answers his cell phone when you call him.
2. He hardly ever answers his cell phone when you are with him.
3. When he does use his cell phone, he talks in a low voice or walks away from you.
4. He only uses his cell phone when you're not around. When you walk into the room or get into the car or truck with him, he hangs up.
5. He stops to go into a store or mall and leaves you in the truck or car, saying he'll only be a minute and there's no need for you to come in with him. Most likely he's returning a call he's missed from his wife or girlfriend.

There are players and hustlers who buy cells just to check their messages for hustling or from their other women. Those other women might even know he's married or in another relationship, but don't care. After these players and hustlers buy extra cell phones, they set up the message that they want to be heard. Then they put the number of the extra cell in their personal cell phone under a fake name. They'll disguise the phone numbers of their other women by using a code that shifts a woman's name to a man's. Kim becomes Keith, Tina or Tonya, Tate, and Gloria or Gaye, George. They will also use coded business names like Kim's Dry Cleaning, Tina's Day Care Service, Gloria's Bakery, or Nikki's Cleaning Service. Or they'll memorize the number, which is safer, because the wife, fiancée, or girlfriend won't be wise to what they're doing when they call to check their messages. Then he'll hide the new cell or pager so you don't know about it. Burner phones he simply throws away when he's used all the minutes.

He's usually worked out a code with the other woman, too. If she calls him, and he starts talking the way he would to a hommie or business associate, she knows his wife or girlfriend is right there and he can't talk, but will call her back when he has a chance.

The player or hustler gives the number of his extra cell or pager to people he doesn't want to have his personal cell phone number. He leaves a message that he'll call back within half an hour or so. That's why he's always checking his cell messages.

Places He Might Hide an Extra Cell Phone

If you suspect your partner has an extra cell, there are a few places you might want to check.

1. In the closet where he keeps his old coats and jackets and the suits he hardly ever wears.
2. Inside old shoes or boots that he never wears anymore.
3. Any extra room where you don't sleep and seldom go.
4. Any area of the house or apartment you're not likely to go, like the basement, attic, or garage.
5. Places where you have seen bugs, mice, or spiders and, he knows, you won't go.
6. Inside his car or truck where he keeps his spare tire and tire jack.

Best Times to Check to See If He Has an Extra Cell

If you're not married or don't' live together, the only time you might be able to find his extra cell phone, if he has one, is when he's at home, at his house or apartment. You would be wasting your time looking for it when he's out of the house or apartment. He's too smart for that; any extra cell phone will be with him wherever he goes. So look when he's around.

1. When he's taking a bath or shower. It's best to look when he's taking a bath. With a shower you only have a few minutes.
2. When he's playing games on his PlayStation or Xbox. He's bound to be playing for at least an hour. This is the best time to look if he's into video games.
3. When he's asleep, but only if he is a heavy sleeper. Then you can get up and look around.

If you've looked and can't find an extra cell phone, it's likely that he doesn't have one or he's hidden it in a very good place. If you do find an extra cell phone or pager, then it's up to you to decide what's best for you to do. But whatever you do, be careful, particularly in how you confront him about what you have found.

You might want to keep the information to yourself to use later when you've had time to think things through and the timing suits you. You need to do what is best for your peace of mind. If he doesn't love you or care about you a little, there's no reason to fight for something he doesn't want as much as you do. What you say or what you do to keep him happy, satisfied, and faithful won't matter to him. He won't change or stop doing his thing with other women or his hustling to make money.

Once you realize that your man is a player, seeing other women, or a hustler, and you stay around and put up with the drama, the headaches, and the heartache, you have no one to blame but yourself. As the old saying goes, "Fool me once, shame on you. Fool me twice, shame on me."

Once you understand the games black men play in their relationships, you have a choice. You don't have to put up with them. You don't have to waste years of your life living a big lie. In your heart you may suspect your partner is not being faithful or is hustling. You may feel it in your gut, but haven't caught him at his games or doing his dirt. By paying attention as the warning signs pile up, you put yourself in a better position to determine whether your suspicions are justified. The black man you love and trust may not be the man you believe he is.

Sexting

Another danger sign that your man might be a player involves sexting, which a lot of black men are doing without their wives, fiancées, or girlfriends knowing. Sexting is like texting, but the messages exchanged are explicit. Men and women send sexy messages or pictures back and forth. Trouble brews when your man starts sharing his sexual fantasies with another woman who's interested in fulfilling his desires. Without you knowing it, your husband, fiancé, or boyfriend might be receiving a sexy text from another woman while you are out to dinner. He could be getting or receiving nude pictures while you're in bed asleep and he's supposedly watching television or playing video games.

Sexting can spice up your sex life by adding a bit of excitement. If it's something that you really want to do, then do it with your partner before another woman does. If you feel your husband, fiancé, or boyfriend isn't paying you as much attention as he did when you first started your relationship, maybe you're not giving him the attention that you used to give him. There are always two sides to a situation so don't point the finger at who's to blame.

Using Sexting to Spice Up Your Love Life

1. Send him a sexy text about your thoughts about him, and what you want to do to him and with him the next time you see him.
2. Send him a sexy text about the sexy dreams you have about him and you both.
3. Send him a sexy text about the desires you have and want to fulfill when you see him later.
4. Send him a sexy text about the fantasies you have about him and you both.
5. Send him a sexy picture of yourself, with a sexy message—"all this is waiting for you when you get home, so hurry up."

You will be surprised how much your partner will love receiving sexy texts from you. The ideal is not to send them too often. As with everything else that brings spice to your love life, you want the sexting message to be a surprise. If you do it all the time, he'll begin to expect the messages and grow tired of them.

Sexting helps build anticipation and is a verbal form of foreplay. Send your husband, fiancé, or boyfriend a sexy text and see how fast he gets home. Once you start texting him, he'll start sending you some about his thoughts, desires, and fantasies about you. Sexting each other can also bring out things about each other that you may not have known before—thoughts about what he likes you to do for him and to him.

By sexting you're helping visualize—what you're wearing and what you're doing—at that moment when you are away from each other. But you want to keep the sexting between the two of you. You need to know if your husband is sexting or having a sexting affair with another woman.

Warning Signs That He Might Be Sexting Another Woman

1. He always goes into a different room to use his cell phone.
2. He suddenly has to go somewhere in his vehicle.
3. He never leaves his cell phone out in the open.
4. You don't know the password to his cell phone. (You share everything else in your relationship. He knows your password, but he won't give you his.)
5. He starts an argument just to have a reason to get out of the house so he can check his text messages.

These are just warning signs, not solid evidence. Always remember to have proof before you accuse a partner of anything. You don't want to look like a fool if you're wrong. There is an easy ploy you can use if you want to make sure your man is being faithful to you when you're not together. Have a female relative or girlfriend he doesn't know call him. See what happens when she says the following:

Hi! My name is____________. You don't remember me, but I met you a few weeks [or months] back at [pick a place you know he goes], and I was wondering if we could meet [hook up] and talk?

Or

Hello! [Use his name] How have you been? I hope you haven't forgotten all about me? [He will most likely ask, "Who's this?"] She'll the give him a fake name and a place that they met [where he goes to get his gas, a haircut, etc.]

You know that this woman is a total stranger to your husband, fiancé, or boyfriend. If he doesn't hang up after the first few seconds of her saying that they had met here or there, you have a major problem with your relationship. If he's willing to meet a woman who is a total stranger, what would he do with a woman that he knows when you're not around?

Few black women want a player or hustler for a husband, fiancé, or boyfriend. They don't want to become victims or statistics. I've watched how players hurt and destroy the lives of so many black women. But being aware of the danger signs and the games that black men play every day and every night, year after year, you can do what's best for you—your peace of mind and your life. Without peace of mind, how happy can you really be?

Chapter 3

Sins of the Father

In a perfect world we would never break each other's hearts. But this isn't a perfect world, far from it. So we need to strive hard with what we are blessed with and never give up on love and happiness.

Black men aren't born players. They are made into players and in two ways: They become players by watching and learning from the black men in their environment as they grow up. Or they become players after women they loved and trusted break their hearts.

I grew up in an environment where my father was a major player and hustler. Why do I call my father a major player, rather than simply a player? Major players are married men who not only cheat and commit adultery, but have another family or families on the side. They play games with their wives and families and with the other women and their children.

The Lies He Tells the Other Woman

1. He's leaving his wife and children in the near future [soon].
2. His wife doesn't make him happy the way she does.
3. His wife doesn't satisfy him as she does.

4. His wife doesn't want to have sex with him anymore and they haven't had sex in months [years].
5. He and his wife sleep in different rooms in their house.
6. All his wife does is argue and fight with him about everything.
7. His wife doesn't want to cook or clean the house anymore and her place is the only one where he can find peace of mind [happiness].
8. He's saving up money to get his own place so his children can come visit him after the divorce.
9. He's leaving his wife and children just as soon as he saves up enough money to hire a good divorce lawyer.
10. He can't leave his wife and children right now. She doesn't have a job, and he's paying all the bills.
11. All his wife does is drink and argue, and he can't deal with it anymore. She's the only thing that keeps him going.
12. Give him a year, or a few years, to make sure his wife and children are okay; then he'll move in with her for good.

These are some of the lies or excuses that major players employ. They want the best of both worlds and will say whatever they need to say to get it.

Many black women believe the lies when they first get involved with a married black man who is a player. But over time their player ways affect and hurt their relationships with their wives and their children; they also damage the other woman and her children.

My father is a good example of a major player. While he was married to my mother, he also had two other families. When I was seventeen, I found out that I had three half-brothers and a half-sister by my father's other women. My cousin went to school with my half- sister. After she discovered that she was my half-sister, he set it up for us to meet. When I met her for the first time, I was dumbfounded. I didn't know what to feel or think. I said hi to her and asked her name and how she was doing. After that, I really didn't know what to say and mumbled that I had to go. When I was saying good-bye, she gave me a big hug. I walked away with all kinds of mixed emotions—hate, anger, and sadness—about what the actions of my father had done to me and my family.

I was totally surprised that I had other brothers and a sister. At that moment everything I had seen and heard between my mother and father started to make sense. I came to understand why we only saw our father a few hours every day when he got off work and hardly ever on weekends. Most of the time we saw him at dinner, but he was out the door after he finished eating.

For a black man to pull off having another family, he has to provide physical, emotional, and financial support to both. If he's financially secure, he can manage the masquerade with ease for many years. Some black men are so good at playing this game that sometimes the wife and her children don't know about the other family until he's on his deathbed or at the funeral service.

Before my best friend's funeral, for example, his mother, wife, and two children (a boy and a girl), and family members gathered at his mother's house to prepare for the services. Out of nowhere, a woman walks in with a little girl and a little boy. She had come to pay respects to her children's father before he was buried. The crazy part of this story was that both the son by his wife and the one by the other woman were named after him (junior).

This pattern happens in black communities more often than is acknowledged. It's something that few people talk about. You'll think your husband, fiancé, or boyfriend is honest and faithful—until he passes away. Then the other woman shows up at your house, the in-laws' house, the funeral parlor, or the church, with her children in tow, to say their good-byes.

Most of the time the wife, fiancée, or girlfriend is the last one to know about the other woman and the children the player had on the side. Growing up, I always thought that my father was out with his friends or hommies. We never knew that we had a half-father in our lives. We had everything that we ever wanted materially, although we never had our father's time—those opportunities to teach us about life or sports, things that every child needs from a father.

Our father hardly ever took us anywhere. I learned everything about life from the streets, my uncles, older male cousins, and older friends or hommies in the neighborhood. My father, I later came to realize, was emotionally weak. He was also broke. To take care of three families, he had to work twelve-hour days and sometimes six or seven days a week. He also turned to hustling. He had to do something extra to make money.

My father started his marriage with cheating already on his mind and in his heart. He never gave his marriage and his family a fighting chance of working and being happy. All four children that he had by the other women were born between me and my two brothers. My half-sister was born a year after me.

Warning Signs that Your Husband, Fiancé, or Boyfriend Might Have Another Family You Don't Know About

There are clues you can look for to find out if your partner has a woman and another family on the side.

1. The amount of money he gives you for the bills, your personal expenses, and the children gets smaller and smaller over the weeks, months, and years.
2. He works a lot of overtime or has gotten another job for extra money, but you don't see the difference in your income. The money he gives you stays basically the same.
3. He is tired a lot more, and he no longer wants to stay up with you at night.
4. He barely eats the food that you cook for him. When he comes home, he tells you that he's not hungry [he's already eaten].
5. He's asleep by the time you get in bed with him, and he doesn't touch you the way he used to.

6. You haven't had sex in weeks or months.
7. Your sex life has changed. Every other night becomes once a week, then every other week, once a month, until you hardly ever have sex. This is a real bad sign if it's been months or years.
8. When you do have sex, the sex is different. There's no passion and the loving feels forced and mechanical to you.
9. He comes in later and later every week and, as time passes, he doesn't get home until morning and he doesn't answer his cell.
10. He seldom spends a whole weekend with you and your children. He usually leaves for a few hours, saying he has to take care of some business or visit a friend, hommie, co-worker, or relative.
11. When he leaves the house, he never offers to take you with him.
12. He never wants to go shopping or out in public places with you or with you and your children. It's as if he doesn't want to be seen with you or the children.
13. He gives you money, but won't give you his car or truck to use to go shopping. When you ask why he can't come with you or let you use the car or truck, he always has an excuse [he has something to do later, etc.].
14. On major holidays, he leaves the house for some reason or another and can't take you or your children with him.

The amount of time your partner spends with you and your partner on the holidays is a major warning sign that he might have another family. On holidays he at least has to show his face even if only for a few hours. If he has other children outside his marriage, for example, he feels he has to be there on Christmas or for birthdays when his other children open their presents.

My father used to be there early in the morning on Christmas when we opened our presents; a few hours later, we'd look around and he'd be gone in the wind, and our mother's mood would change from happy to sad to angry. When she noticed I was watching her, she would do her best to hide her feelings.

I realized later that my mother knew my father was going to see his other families. Sitting at the top of the stairs one day, I overheard her talking on the phone. But she never said anything while we were around. She was too afraid of our father. For a long time I kept silent. When I finally asked her why she didn't get a divorce, she told me that she stayed with him because she knew she wouldn't get any child support from him if she left him. When my youngest brother graduated from high school, she filed for divorce.

My father, I realize, must have been under a lot of pressure, trying to be in three places at once and living a lie. The news of his other families affected each of us differently. I lost a lot of love and respect for him and went on with my life, trying to be my own man and promising myself that I would never be the father or husband that he was. My younger brother adapted a lot better than I did and accepted that he had a half-sister and three half-brothers.

My youngest brother took the discovery the hardest; he swore he never wanted to see our father again, that he hated him for what he had done to our family. He felt our father had abandoned us. But in reality our father had abandoned us emotionally many years before our mother divorced him. He just used our home as a place to eat and sleep. When I look back on my teenage years, I realize that my father never gave me advice when I got into any trouble. All I got was punishment and hell when I stepped out of line.

After my youngest brother found out my father had two other families, he started to get into trouble with the law. Then he signed up for the Navy. While he was in the Navy, he married and had two sons. All the time he was married, however, he was also in a relationship with another woman and had two sons with her. In effect, he became the mirror image of our father—the man he said he hated for having another family. My brother had become the man our father was. He now has eight children—two sons by his ex-wife,

the way we should. Other races in America look out for their own people.

It's sad that we as black men are against each other now. Take the statistics for homicides today. In metropolitan cities and even small towns black men are killing black men. We're killing each other off like it's going out of style, and we blame white America for a lot of things that happen to us. White America is far from innocent, but the majority of the time it's black men who are killing black men and black women. We as black men are out of control with our hate and envy for one another.

As a black man, I have come to realize, black men have to think twice, sometimes three times, in a lot of situations before we act or say anything. Once we act on something, there's almost nothing we can do to fix it or take it back. Once a life has been taken, there's nothing you can do or say, no matter how sorry you are or how much you regret your actions. If you steal from a man, you can apologize and give him back what you stole. If you break something of that man's, you can apologize and replace it or give him money for the value of the item. If you take that man's life, however, you can never give it back, no matter what you say or do.

I apologize for this digression, but it sickens me how black men are killing each other off every day and every night, 365 days a year. I believe with all my heart that the lack of black fathers in black boys' lives growing up leads to the disrespect that we have in our black communities. Major players and hustlers bear responsibility here. Their lack of commitment and caring gets passed on to the next generation—to their sons—and the cycle of multiple families repeats itself. Reading the warning signs, black women—at least some black women—may be able to alter the pattern and kick the player or hustler out or, better yet, never get involved with him in the first place.

Chapter 4

It's As If They're Playing a Game

Real love deepens and enriches every part of your life.
So why settle for less, black women?

Many black men treat their relationships and marriages like games to be played. It's as if they were acting in a movie—with them as the star, working from a script with faked emotions and faked intentions. These men stay in character until they get what they want out of you. Then they show their true selves.

No matter how good an actor the individual man might be or how tight a game he plays, one day he is going to get tired of acting the part of a loving, honest, faithful, caring man. That's when his true feelings and real intentions come out. After he gets what he wants from you he'll show you his real face, his true self. Most likely he'll do this when he finds another woman, another victim, to use and prey on to satisfy his new need and wants.

Not everything a black man does is about getting into your panties. A lot of times black men want more from you than sex. Although sex is the main thing a man wants from a woman, black men have other reasons for continuing to use women after they've had sex with them.

A black woman who is sexually involved with a black man is usually sensitive to his needs and situation. Why? Women are compassionate by nature. Being a beautiful, loving, understanding black woman, you're going to feel some concern for his dilemma, his situation, and want to offer to help in small or big ways—sometimes financially. That's the kind of women black women are—caring, understanding, loving and supportive—when it comes to the men in their lives. And that's what a lot of black men who are players are looking for; they will use your compassionate side to try and take advantage of you.

Some players will try to move in with you. Only weak players come right out and ask for help or to move in. The real player never asks. His game is too tight for that. He would rather make up difficulties, play on your sympathies, hoping you'll offer to help him out until he gets back on his feet. He will slide his living or financial situation into a conversation with you or let you overhear an exchange when he's talking about it on the phone with someone else. Obviously he hopes that you'll suggest that he move in with you or that you'll give him money until he can turn things around. He knows you're loving and caring and will do that if you can.

A player uses his situation as a ploy. He'll tell you stories about his living circumstances until you start feeling sympathetic. By now you feel comfortable with him. Every time he comes over to visit or spend some time with you, he helps out around your place with the cooking and cleaning. He even fixes things without being asked. The next thing you know, you're asking him to move in with you.

Alarm bells should sound if you've only know him a few weeks and he's already telling you about all the trouble he's having finding a job and paying his bills, but, judging from his clothes, car or truck, and bar bill, he doesn't look as if he's hurting for money.

Things a Player Might Do or Say When He Wants to Move in with You

1. He's living with a friend or relative. They don't get along, so he's looking for a place of his own.

2. He doesn't like where he lives and is planning to move before his next month's rent is due.
3. He invites you to go apartment hunting with him, just to show you how sincere he is about finding another place to live. He'll even bring the real estate section from a newspaper or apartment rental books.

The Real Reason He Has to Move

1. He has a lot of overdue bills and his rent is due. He has to move before being evicted or the bill collectors catch up with him.
2. The woman he lives with is tired of dealing with his lies and games and wants him out of her place and life.
3. He lives with a relative who wants him to find his own place because he no longer helps out with the bills or rent.

After you ask him to move in with you, he'll offer or promise to pay at least half the bills. Here is where you separate the lies from the truth. If he's a good man, he'll live up to his promise. If he's a player, over time he'll contribute less and less until he's giving you nothing at all.

Knowledge is priceless, and it's better to discover early whether the new man you're getting involved with is a player or worse—before you fall too deeply in love with him. Love is blind and can make it hard to see the truth, even when it's right in front of your face.

Being burned by a player or hustler can sour your perspective. It's easy to assume that all black men are out for what they can get. That's a big mistake. A lot of black men *really* are trying to get back on their feet without any help. For example, you may be starting a relationship with a black man who seems to be honest and sincere, but you are suspicious, given the lies you've heard and heartache you've been through. He doesn't have a car or truck and you keep waiting for him to ask to borrow yours. But he doesn't. Instead, he does whatever it takes to get to work or find a job. To get to work or a job interview, he walks, catches a bus or train, or hitches a ride with friends because he's independent and wants to make it on his own.

It's okay for you to let this kind man use your car or truck so long as it doesn't interfere with your work schedule—at least until he gets his own vehicle. You shouldn't let the actions, lies, and games of the black men who have been in your life blind you when you find a good black man who is sincere about beginning a relationship with you. (If you are going to let any man—good or player—use your vehicle, be sure to list him as a designated driver on your insurance. If you don't and he gets into an accident, then it's going to cost you more than some tears.)

The attitude the black man you are involved with has toward your vehicle is another warning sign of whether or not he is a player. When you first let a player or hustler use your car or truck, he will return it promptly, right on schedule. Then, as the weeks pass, he will bring it back later, sometimes much later, than he said he would.

Excuses You Might Hear from Him

1. I didn't notice it was so late. I was busy taking care of business [although he leaves unspecified just what that business was].
2. I didn't know it was that late; it won't happen again. [But it does happen, again and again.]
3. I forgot that I had to stop by the store to get a few things before I came home. [He'll even bring shopping bags home to cover up the reason he's so late.]
4. I got a phone call from my friend, hommie, or relative and had to stop by his place before I brought your vehicle back.
5. I had to give my friend, hommie, or relative a ride because his car or truck was acting up.

6. The football game, basketball game, or championship fight went on a lot longer than I thought it would.

A good man, by contrast, would bring your car or truck back to you promptly, with a full tank of gas, or at least one close to full. He will sometimes return it washed and cleaned, inside and out. And he will offer to drive you wherever you want or need to go.

How a Player Treats Your Car or Truck When You Let Him Use It

1. He will bring your vehicle back to you with hardly any gas left in the tank and offer thin excuses: I didn't notice the gauge was almost on empty or I didn't have any money to fill the tank up.
2. When he returns your vehicle, it reeks of weed, even though he told you when you first met that he didn't get high or smoke.
3. He leaves your car or truck in a mess, with garbage and wrappers all over the seats.

Then you start to notice other differences after he drives your car or truck. The passenger seat has been pulled back or pushed forward, and is not in the position you left it in. The interior smells of a cologne or perfume you don't wear. Then you find female items that are not yours—a lipstick, say. (The other woman will sometimes leave her personal things around intentionally out of spite or to cause trouble. She knows the car belongs to you.)

How a black man treats your place and your vehicle tells you a lot and can help you distinguish between a player or hustler and a good man. The good man's honesty and intentions come through in his actions, not just his words. Words don't mean a thing unless they are put into action. If you remember that, you will be a much happier woman.

Chapter 5

Have to Have Him No Matter What It Takes

If that love is meant for you, it will never leave you. But if it's not, there's nothing on earth that will help you keep it, no matter how hard you try.

Sometimes a woman gets pregnant and has a child or children by the man she loves to hold on to him, or to keep him faithful, or to push him into leaving his wife or other girlfriend, or just to keep him around. But no matter how much you may love him or how badly you want him in our life, getting pregnant won't make him love you and be faithful if he doesn't already love you. It may slow him down, but that's all.

Some men do change and become faithful, but usually they already had true feelings before the pregnancy. If he's a major player and he was deep into playing his games when you met him, the odds are against you.

Playing the game of lies and deceit is like taking drugs, and you get more addicted the longer you play. Just as it's hard to give up alcohol or cigarettes after drinking or smoking for years, it's hard to quite being a player.

Habits are difficult to break. A player can get so good at the game and it makes him feel so good that he just doesn't want to stop. When he's playing in the game, he's not thinking about getting caught or hurting his wife or girlfriend. All he knows is that it gives him pleasure, makes him feel like a real man.

Playing in the game is like playing a sport against other players who are out there on the streets. If you watch closely enough, you can see the game being played in your work place, on the streets, at the mall, in supermarkets, night clubs, and sports bars. A black man will catch you just walking down the street or waiting for a bus and say something real nice, real smooth, to get you interested and then spin his best lines to try and impress you. He wants you to open up and give him your name and, he hopes, your phone number or at least get you to take his number.

We all know that the black man with the best lines gets the attention and a lot of times the phone number as well. He sparks your interest and you want to see where it might lead. The same goes for black women who are players. They dress in sexy outfits, wear bling-bling, and tool around in fancy vehicles to attract men.

The only time a lot of black men stop playing the game is when they fall in love, when they are really into their wives or girlfriends. They realize before it's too late that staying in the game will jeopardize their relationships. Then there are the black men who stop playing only after it brings drama to their lives. They come to understand that it's not worth the hurt and pain it might cause either their wives or girlfriends—or them

But the major players will continue to play games no matter what happens or who gets emotionally or physically damaged. They never stop or change their ways. They are as addicted to playing as heavy drinkers or smokers are to alcohol and tobacco. It satisfies them too much to stop, or they're too weak, or they just don't care about themselves or anyone else in their lives to be concerned about what their behavior might cost.

That's how a lot of black men think and feel about playing in the game. They can't or won't stop playing. Always remember to trust your gut feelings. Often you'll find out later that they were right. But check your suspicions against the facts, with concrete information o whether your husband or boyfriend is playing games and only wants sex from you.

A lot of black women don't mind sharing another woman's husband or boyfriend. In my interviews, many black women told me they don't want to be alone. They need someone to hold them at night and refuse to be by themselves. If they have to share another woman's husband or boyfriend, then that's what they're willing to do. Black women like these make it easier for black men to play games in their marriages and relationships. They also make it harder for black women who want their own husbands or boyfriends and don't want to share.

Most of the women that I talked to about sharing another woman's husband or boyfriend said it was the man's job to make sure that the wife or girlfriend didn't find out about the arrangement. But these women need to think carefully about how many women they are sharing him with. They very well might not be his only side dish.

No matter what anyone tells you, black women always have a choice: They can decide whether or not they are going to deal with black men who play games. But the trick is to identify the men who are players. Not everything is always what it seems to be when it comes to dealing with players.

I didn't write this book to bust your bubble or mess up your dreams of Mr. Perfect. But you need to know the truth about the games that are being played every day and night all around you. Before you start having sex or getting pregnant, you need to know if the guy is a player without any real emotional commitment. Having a baby to keep a guy who's not worth keeping is just plain stupid. Besides it probably won't work any way if the guy's a major player.

Choices, informed choices, can be made before a marriage or relationship gets out of control and causes a lot of headaches and heartache. There's no price for peace of mind and heart—even if that peace means being alone for a spell.

Chapter 6

A Dangerous Game

It's always better to be safe than sorry later.

Everything, I've said, isn't always what it seems to be, particularly when it comes to what your husband or boyfriend does for a living or to make money. A lot of black men work overtime or take on extra jobs, and there's still not enough money. So they do a little hustling on the side to stay above water on the monthly bills or to make life better for themselves and their families.

Other black men act as if they're going to work every day or every night when they're really out there hustling to make extra money. Then you have the straight-up hustlers who hustle for a living and their women don't care so long as they're being taken care of.

The problem comes when the black man is hustling and doesn't let his wife or girlfriend know what he really does to make money. If she knew, she would at least have a choice about whether or not she wanted to deal with his life style and the way he makes his money.

My first experiences with hustling came from the streets and my father when I was around twelve. One morning before going to school, I went into my parents' bedroom to use the cologne my father kept on top of the dresser. The girls at school liked the way I smelled when I wore it. On the way over to dresser, I kicked something under my parents' bed. Being curious, I looked underneath the bed and found a big plastic shopping bag.

My father disliked us being in his bedroom; he knew exactly how everything was before he left the house. I did my best to memorize how the shopping bag had been arranged before I pulled it out. I found four ziplock plastic bags filled to the top with marijuana. I took a handful of weed out of each ziplock; then I slid the shopping bag back underneath the bed exactly as I had found it, praying that my father wouldn't notice the weed no longer went all the way to the top of the ziplocks. He didn't and that's how I first got into hustling and selling drugs in school and around my neighborhood. Growing up, my other male relatives were hustling too, but I didn't know then that the extra money they were making came from selling drugs or that they needed to hustle to take care of their other women and children.

If my father had been faithful and had just one family to take care of, my brothers, mothers, and I would have had better and happier lives, at least my mother would have been happier. My father most likely wouldn't have had to sell drugs and hustle to make the extra money needed to take care of all his women and children. I am not sure if my mother knew my father was selling drugs. But one day I plan to ask her whether she knew, all those years she was married, that he sold drugs and kept them under the bed that they both slept in.

Many black women who are married or in relationships don't have a clue what their husbands or boyfriends do to make money. It's almost impossible for a marriage or relationship to survive when your husband or boyfriend is spreading himself thin with working, hustling, and taking care of other women and their children. There's nothing left for your marriage or your relationship to grow from or build on. Any marriage or relationship needs five things to survive and succeed: love trust, honesty, communication, and time. Without them, a marriage is bound to fail. That's what happened to my parents' marriage, my brothers' marriages, and my marriage. They were missing one, two, three, four or all of these five elements.

How can trust or honesty develop when you don't know what your partner does to make money? You need to know not only to help your relationship grow, but to ensure that you and your family don't get caught up in something you can't get out of. Many black women have been used by black men and realize it only when drama comes into their lives.

Several years ago a young black woman was going to college in Ohio. She met a nice smooth-talking black man that she liked. Without really knowing anything about him, she gave him the keys to her place and her body because she liked him. Then one day she was arrested on her way to class. She was later indicted for conspiracy in drug trafficking and incarcerated. It turns out she was in a relationship with a major drug dealer. The federal government also indicted her boyfriend and others that she didn't even know.

She tried to explain to the federal agents that she didn't know her boyfriend was selling drugs, but they didn't believe her. They had evidence that he had given her thousands of dollars, paid for her college classes, and bought her expensive jewelry and a fancy car. She told them that she thought he had a lot of money because he ran a successful business.

To make a long and sad story short, the judge and jury didn't buy her story, and she was sentenced to twenty-six years. The last I heard she was waiting on an answer to her appeal. To a black man familiar with hustling and the games black men play, her story is not only believable in ways a judge and jury couldn't fathom; it is probably true. I've been in relationships in the past where I was hustling to make extra money and the woman I was with had no idea what I was doing behind her back to make money. But when I was hustling I never brought anything home; that was rule number-one for me. But a lot of black men don't follow that rule because it's all about them and what they can get; they don't care who gets hurt in the process.

News reports often run stories of black males, black females, and even whole black families being murdered in drug-related crimes. Black men bring a lot of dirt from the streets into their homes when they are hustling. And sometimes, when they're selling drugs or guns, that dirt washes over innocent women and children.

Although I hesitate to judge what anyone does to make money, any woman in a marriage or relationship has the right to know what is going on. Only then can she protect herself and her children or make an informed decision to ride with the way he's making money. A woman might not say anything because he's bringing her a lot of money, buying a brand-new car, furs, designer clothes, or bling to wear. But when the drama comes, and you're facing a lot of time away from your children, family, and friends, it's too late. The price may not be worth the material things you received from him.

The drama often comes with a steep price. A black woman who owned her own apartment building fell in love with a black man who was renting one of her units. She was also living in the building with her daughter. After she got involved with the man, she was arrested and indicted for drug conspiracy. Federal agents said there was no way for her not to know that her boyfriend was selling drugs in the building. She denied any knowledge of his drug dealing, but the court didn't believe her and sentenced her to 185 months. She was thirty-two and left her teenage daughter to be raised by her grandmother. Freedom is priceless, and a lot of us don't realize how precious until it's taken away. It's always better to be safe than sorry for the rest of your life. Be vigilant and follow up on your instincts.

Warning Signs That He Might Be Hustling Behind Your Back

1. He hardly ever comes home when he tell you he'll be home.
2. He receives or has to make phone calls on his cell phone at crazy hours in the early morning.
3. He leaves the room where you are to talk on his cell phone.

4. He receives phone calls from men and women whose names you have never heard before.
5. When you ask him who called, he gives you some weak explanation or avoids answering.
6. He has to leave the apartment or house at the last minute to take care of business even though he told you earlier he was in for the night.
7. He often gets picked up at your apartment or house by different men or women in different vehicles.
8. He has a lot of money around the apartment or house, more than usual.
9. He gives you more money for bills and for yourself than he did before and, as far as you know, he doesn't have another job and hasn't been working any overtime.
10. He puts a safe in the apartment or house and tells you it's a place to keep his valuables and important papers in case of a fire. But he never gives you the combination or the key.
11. He's buying a lot of new clothes and jewelry for himself and you.
12. He buys a new car or truck for himself and for you. When you ask him how you can afford them, he tells you that he hit the street number or won the money gambling—which may be true every now and then, but not every other week.

Don't jump the gun and assume that your husband or boyfriend is hustling because he occasionally gives you a lot of money. The tipoff is when it's a lot of money almost every day or week for a year or so when you know he doesn't run his own business and only works forty hours a week, if that. Take mental notes and tally them with what he has told you. Over time you will learn a lot if you pay close attention. When you feel that things don't add up, it's time to have a heart-to-heart face-to-face. Maybe he can clear up your doubts with some logical explanation or maybe he'll come clean and be honest with you, and just maybe he won't.

Each situation is different and so are the black men you are dealing with in your relationships. A lot of women ignore the signs and warnings that they see every day. That's a dangerous tactic. Once aware of the games that black men play, you can use that awareness and be prepared when a partner tries a game on you. It's up to you to use what you know to get to the truth. You can at the least put to rest the doubts you have been having or confirm them.

Chapter 7

With More Money Come More Problems

The more money a player has, the more games he can get away with playing because money cleans up the dirt.

More money can solve certain problems in a relationship, but not when a player, flush with cash, uses that money to hide the dirt or wash it away. Black men who are the biggest players are the entertainers, professional athletes, or successful businessmen. Why? Because they have the money to maintain more than one relationship with ease.

Not all black entertainers, professional athletes, or business executives are players, but a lot of them are. And they have some of the very best excuses when they're playing. They can easily use pressing business or the demands of a tour or road trip to explain why they can't make it home for the night or until tomorrow.

Scenes in the movie *Love & Basketball* illustrate what I'm talking about. The husband, a professional basketball star, consistently blames his absences on the demands of his career: he has a meeting with big team executives after his basketball games to discuss his career or his future when he retires. The meetings are all scheduled at night or during a road trip and he can't fly back home. All the time, he is using his career as an excuse to cover up his affairs with other women. He even has another child by one of the many women he is seeing. Stories like these crop up all the time in the newspapers and gossip rags.

The entertainment, sports, or business worlds never sleep. If your husband or boyfriend is involved in them, he can have a business meeting with anyone about anything at any time of the day or night. Money talks, and black men are going to go where the money is and meet with whomever they need to see to make it.

Many black women who are married or involved with men in these fields know what's going on, but don't say anything about the playing as long as their men take care of the bills and keep their playing ways away from home or out of the news. The old saying, "What you don't know won't hurt you," is not always true. Take the example of Magic Johnson, who played for the L.A. Lakers and caught the HIV virus. Fortunately he didn't give it to his wife. But, unhappily, there are a lot of not-so-fortunate wives and girlfriends who have been infected with STDs or HIV by their partners.

When I was studio manager at Platinum Bound Records, aka Team PB, in Philadelphia, my job required me to open the studio and set up studio time for different artists in the music business. I arranged meetings with different artists to host parties at night clubs and after parties and then managed the events throughout Pennsylvania and the tri-state area. I did everything from finding talent, introducing them to the production team at the studio, to overseeing the money collected and paying staff and the owners of the night clubs our studio rented for shows.

Behind closed doors, I did much more. As studio manager my primary responsibility was to keep the artists, who were paying for studio time, happy, comfortable, and in the studio for a long as I could. The longer they stayed, the more money we made. I would order whatever food or drinks they wanted, buy blunts and weed if we didn't already have it at the studio—and not any kind of marijuana, only the city's very best.

If the artists wanted women with them in the studio, I'd call women we knew who were into keeping artists company for the thrill of it or having sex with them for money. I'd pick up an artist from the airport, hotel, or night club and lie for him when his wife or girlfriend called the studio looking for him. If an artist wasn't there or had a woman with him, I was asked to tell the wife or girlfriend that he was in the recording booth or overseeing a closed recording session. Then I would tell him what I had told his wife or girlfriend so he'd know what to say when he talked to her later.

Everyone wants to be a part of the music business. It's glamorous and goes hand in hand with everything else these days. There's nothing that it doesn't touch or influence. And the patterns in the music business, the behavior, carry over to other spheres of the entertainment business, professional sports, and corporate America.

There is a simple way to find out whether or not the black man in your life who is an entertainer, professional athlete, or successful businessman is also a player. Next time he has to go out of town, ask him whether you can go with him. If he says okay, it's a good sign that he's not a player. But be wary if he takes a while before telling you no or gives you any of the following excuses or objections.

1. Who's going to watch the children if you go?
2. It's too late to get a plane ticket for you. Maybe next time you can come.
3. He's going to be gone for more than a few days, maybe even weeks. It's impossible for you to be away that long.
4. You have to work.
5. You have places to take the children this week.
6. He has a lot of business meetings planned and won't be able to spend time with you if you come along.
7. You'll be bored if you come. Stay home and do some shopping. He'll take you on a trip or vacation when he gets back.

After he gives you any of these excuses or raises any of these objections, insist on going with him. You want to test his reactions, and the way he handles your persistence will give you valuable clues. The harder he tries to keep you from accompanying him on his trip, the more likely it is that he is a player. It's a bad sign if you get into an argument or he flies off the handle after you ask to go along on a trip. Guilt is the root of a lot of arguments in relationships. Often your partner will start an argument or get mad as a distraction. He would rather have you upset with him for a few days than to have you catch him cheating or finding out about his other woman or children.

After the argument, your husband or boyfriend will try to make up with you.

1. He'll buy you something expensive—jewelry, furs, a new car or truck.
2. He'll make plans for that romantic trip or vacation you've been wanting to take for months or years.
3. He will offer to take you on a shopping spree or give you his black card to go crazy and buy whatever you want.

Players who are rich can make big gestures when you're mad. Players who don't have that kind of money settle for dinner at an expensive restaurant, a night of dancing at a nice club, flowers, small bling, or a card.

If your husband or boyfriend keeps telling you there's no way that you can come with him on his trip, find out, before he leaves, the name of the hotel where he'll be staying. It's a bad sign if he hasn't volunteered the information already, but a good one if he tells you without prompting just in case you need or want to get in touch. Ninety-eight percent of the black women I've talked to and interviewed believe that being able to communicate with your mate or loved one is one of the most important things in a marriage or relationship.

If you have real grounds for thinking your partner may be playing around when he's away, if there's a suspicious pattern in his behavior, after you get the information about where he's staying, give him time to check in. If you don't hear from him after a few hours after his plane has landed, call his cell phone. If he doesn't answer, call his room or suite at the hotel. If you still don't get an answer, you can either make a mental note of the situation or you can get someone to watch your children and catch the next flight to the city where he's staying.

Once you arrive, try to get a room on the same floor, but don't show yourself. If you're wrong about you suspicions, you can jump back on a plane home, and he won't know that you have been checking up on him while he was away.

Karrine Steffans, in her book *Confessions of a Video Vixen*, talks about how the black men in the entertainment business and professional athletes played games with her while they were in relationships with their wives or girlfriends. The book shows how rich black men can play the game better than anyone; if you haven't read it, you should.

One of my favorite rap songs is Jay-Z's "Song Cry." The song tells a story: He has a good woman in his corner, that he loves, who loves him and has had his back from the beginning of their relationship. Then he becomes successful and starts paying her less and less attention. The more money he makes and the more famous he becomes, the more women want to be with him and he's spending little time with her. One day she gets tired of the games he's playing and leaves him to go back home.

The song is soul stirring, It makes you realize that black men—blinded by pretty faces, sexy bodies, and the money—can take love for granted until it is too late. But once the party's over and the smoke clears, many look around for their true heart and realize the love they once had all to themselves is gone. But that choice was Jay-Z's woman's to make, too. With her eyes wide open, she made the decision to leave. It's important for black women to keep their eyes open, read the warning signs and make those decisions for themselves—to take control of their lives.

Chapter 8

It's a Different World

Be careful of the smiling faces of those who call you friend and never take for granted that they won't step into your shoes.

The twenty-first century has brought a different attitude among a lot of younger black women. They don't give a damn if a man is married or has a fiancé or girlfriend. They'll step right up to him when his wife or girlfriend turns away. Some are so bold that they'll whisper in his ear their names and phone numbers with his wife or girlfriend standing right there. Many of the women with this "I don't care" attitude have husbands or boyfriends. These are the female players, who are deep into the game and make it easier for a man who has a wife or girlfriend to play the game.

Some call them groupies. What's a groupie? A groupie is not just a woman who is into dating or seeing entertainers and professional athletes. She's the type of woman who will roll solo or team up with other women who are also players. She goes to night clubs or sports events to catch the attention of black athletes or successful businessmen who hang out there. Any place a celebrity or prominent man typically goes without his wife or girlfriend will do. She wants to catch him with his guard down and preferably a little intoxicated.

A lot of groupies are out for the money and what they can get, but they love the sex too. It's all part of the game to them, just as it is for the male players. Some people call them tricks, gold diggers, or hustlers rather than groupies; it all depends on the perspective. Their radar is set to home in on singers, rappers, entertainers, professional athletes, or drug dealers—anyone in the V.I.P. section of night clubs or drives a flashy car, wears expensive jewelry or ice, and buys up the bar.

For years I ran night clubs as well as after parties for singers and rappers like Miss J, Nelly, Cash Money Millionaires, N.O.R.E., Naughty by Nature, State Property, Ram Squad, Philly's Most Wanted, and E.S.T. (the Greatest Man Alive), to name a few, and have watched groupies size a man up and go after their victim with a vengeance. Sometimes I felt sorry for the black man because these women pulled no punches. They held nothing back to get what they wanted from the man. If the man was a player himself, he couldn't resist this kind of woman. He was in the game already and playing it with female players challenged his ego and his skills.

The night clubs and music scene are different worlds. They won't affect women who have strong marriages or relationships. But the club culture and the music scene can do significant damage to a relationship that is already weak. If your relationship is on shaky ground, try to prevent your partner from going to night clubs or sports bar by himself. You'll need finesses, sweetness, and some skill, but black women, when they set their minds to it, know how to get their partners to do almost anything. If you can't stop him from going, go with him and bring along a sister, a cousin, or girlfriends.

When I first started managing night clubs, among my other duties, I was in charge of the security staff and the V.I.P. section of the club. In the night club business, you have to watch everyone from the parking valets to the bartender because many are out to make extra money on the side. After a Nelly concert, I was managing the after party for Nelly. The security staff we'd hired was out of New York and was letting people in through the kitchen. They were charging double the price and didn't check IDs.

I discovered their scam when two under-aged sisters confessed they had come in with their cousin through the back door. They said they would have paid triple to meet Nelly. While I was talking to them, Nelly walked by, headed for the men's restroom. The older of the two sisters gestured to her sister: "There he goes, go get him." The younger sister followed Nelly straight into the men's room. Nelly came right out; a minute or so later the younger sister followed, looking upset. What happened? the older sister asked. But her younger sibling didn't want to talk about it. I assumed that things hadn't gone according to plan, but the incident reveals the lengths to which a groupie or female hustler will go to catch the eye of a man—particularly a celebrity's or a rich man's.

After that night I started watching everyone and everything like a hawk. I soon realized a lot of people were having sex in the V.I.P sections, dark corners, restrooms, or the cars parked in the lot outside. I also noticed that the unisex restrooms were the most notorious spots in the night clubs; people were having sex in them as if it was going out of style. Some of these night clubs were like strip clubs, with private dark booths. Black men that I knew and worked with would come up to me and ask if I had any condoms so they could have sex in the club with someone they had just met or with someone they had made plans to meet beforehand.

One night I was working a night club and I met this very sexy woman. She was with her girlfriends at the bar area where I was waiting for my drink. She came up to me, smiling and flirting as if we were long-lost friends. She asked if I'd mind buying her a drink. I didn't mind and offered to buy her girlfriends drinks as well. It seemed only fair since they were all together. We ended up talking, laughing, drinking, and dancing together.

While dancing with her back to me, she ground her butt all over me; she took my hand and moved it underneath her skirt so I could feel that she didn't have any panties on. Next she was trying to get in my zipper, telling me that she hadn't had any dick in a long time.

It was jam packed on the dance floor and so dark no one would have noticed anything. But I just couldn't—not because I didn't want to. She was crazy sexy, smelled so good, and felt even better next to me, and I wasn't in a relationship. But I didn't have any protection, and I wasn't having sex raw with any women, no matter how sexy she was. She got upset and went off looking for someone who would. I didn't care because I'd rather be safe than sorry later. I didn't know her from a can of paint.

Another time while I was managing another night club, I walked into the men's room and saw two black men having their way with a half-naked woman while other men watched. They were doing their thing, as if was nothing new and they didn't care who was watching.

A few months later, working yet another club, I took a break from the club's cash window where I collected the money. I needed to warm myself up. We left the front door open to let people in and it was freezing at the cash window. On the way to the bar, I ran into a sexy young black woman who wanted me to dance with her. No sooner had we hit the dance floor than she was all over me. Even before I knew her name, she was asking me if I would like to be her Sugar Daddy. At first I thought I had heard her wrong. So I screamed into her ear to repeat what she'd said. She looked at me in confusion, and then told me that she really needed a man to take care of her and her bills. She'd do whatever I wanted whenever I wanted it. I was so caught off guard that I started laughing.

As you can see, a lot more goes on in night clubs than drinking, getting high, and dancing. If you have an honest, faithful man in your life, you don't have to worry when he goes to night clubs without you. But if your partner has not passed the majority of the tests I've mentioned, you should be concerned about what he might get up to or be urged to do in a club.

Similarly, not everything that goes on in a recording studio or closed session is about recording music. Artists, managers, producers, DJs, and radio hosts use recording studios as places to rendezvous with their other women or girlfriends, and women they meet at concerts, night clubs, or promotional events. I've watched men send their wives or girlfriends and their children home, saying they're having a late night, a closed session, and won't be home until late.

Everyone in the music business knows that the longer you keep an artist recording in the studio the more work they'll get done and the more money they'll spend and make. The wives and girlfriends know this and don't question it when their husband or boyfriends tell them they have to leave the studio.

If the artist's wife or girlfriend asks to stay for the session, most of the time he'll tell her he doesn't want her around all the drinking, weed smoking, cursing and crazy behavior that goes on during a lot of closed sessions. Or he'll tell her that the others don't want anyone around but their people or entourage. This is often the case with the big names. They don't want anyone to know that they're in the city.

Some in the music business use the pretext of a closed session to meet their other women. The recording room is generally equipped with love seats, sofas, chairs, and futons to relax on—and to have sex on. Most music studios also have showers, so cleaning up is easy.

Recording studios are soundproof and usually cell phones can't receive a signal. As a result, a wife or girlfriend can get in touch with her husband or boyfriend only through the studio's phone. Whoever is in charge of answering the studio's phone will be instructed to tell anyone who calls that he is in a closed session and can't come to the phone or be disturbed. If his wife or girlfriend tries to surprise him by dropping by the studio unannounced, they can see who's at the door on the security cameras and won't answer the door when she rings the bell. If she tries to call the studio's phone while standing at the door or sitting in her car in front of the studio, they'll let the answering machine pick up.

I'm not going to get into what goes on in a lot of closed sessions or the dark rooms of night clubs. I just wanted to give you a little insight into how easy it is for someone rich or in the sports or entertainment worlds to be a big-time player without his wife or girlfriend knowing. Any woman caught in this situation can, however, take time to understand the environment in which her man works and to understand the abundant opportunities he has to cheat. That awareness, that understanding, she can then use to make it more difficult even for a hard-core player to cheat or to make it clear, as Jay-Z's woman did, that she won't put up with the games.

Chapter 9

Always Protect Your Neck

If you have doubts about something or someone, hold on to those feelings and trust yourself. Life is too short for guessing, and there's no coming back from something once it happens. Protect yourself. Always be aware of your surroundings and keep around you not just those you think you can trust, but those you know you can trust from their past actions.

The night club scene has changed radically over the last few years with the introduction of the different date-rape drug that can be bought on any street corner and with the aggressive attitudes of today's black men who have been drinking heavily or smoking weed before they even get to a club.

Lax security compounds the problems. Any known musician, athlete, or celebrity can get into a club without being searched. The hustlers—male and female—slip security anywhere from fifty to a few hundred dollars to get in without being searched. Supposedly that's how the rap artist C-Murder snuck into a club the weapon he used to kill an under-age teenager in a club restricted to those over twenty-one.

To make extra money, security staff will let in under-age kids and not search anyone. They will use their walkie talkies to let the other security staff know that they are sending folks around back and what to charge them when they get there. They may even have worked up a fee schedule for groups.

Whenever you go out to a night club, no matter where it might be, try not to go by yourself unless you know someone who works at the club. Take at least one other woman with you. There's safety and protection in numbers—the more the better. And always remember that looks can be deceiving. That man smiling at you may actually be sizing you up as his next prey or victim.

When I was a studio manager, I was in charge of managing some of the nicest, and the wildest, night clubs in Philadelphia and the tri- state area. One time, Platinum Bound Records aka Team PB had a small concert with radio hosts (DJs) from Power 99 in Philadelphia. The concert headliner was Philly's Most Wanted. Da Sinisters opened the show; after performing three songs, they left the stage, and we all took a break while they set up for E.S.T., who were performing next.

I went to the bar with the rest of our studio team. That's when I was approached by a pretty black woman—young and petite—and her female cousin. She couldn't wait to tell me that it was her birthday; she had just turned twenty-one. It was also the first time she'd been to a night club to see a rap concert performed live. Her excitement was contagious. She couldn't stop talking about how this was the best day of her life. She could drink and dance whenever she wanted. After treating her to a celebratory glass of champagne and chatting a little more, she went off to dance and I got back to work.

The next glimpse I got of her, she's wedged between two black men who were trying to rape her right there on the dance floor inside a packed club. They were acting like fiends, tearing at her clothes as if she was a piece of meat. One fool had her blouse wide open. She didn't have a bra on, and he was groping her breasts, while the other fiend was grinding on her from the back. She was all of 5'4" in her high heels and might have weighed 105 pounds.

I was mad as hell when I saw what these grown men were doing to her. I could see the fear and shock in her eyes. By the time I got to them, she was barely fighting anymore. The music was blasting so loud you couldn't hear anyone if they were standing right next to you screaming for help and she was so small in-between those two fiends that you could barely see her. If we hadn't talked when she first came into the club, I might have walked right by without noticing her.

Once I reached her, I knew she was in trouble. Just then she saw me and held out her hand for help. I grabbed it and started pulling her toward me. One of the fiends noticed what I was doing and shouted at me: "What the fuck are you doing?" I screamed back. "She's with me." I could see by the expression in his eyes that he didn't believe me.

After a brief tug of war with the fiends, I pulled her into my arms. Then, out of nowhere, a few members of my crew popped up and stared down the fiends, who quickly retreated and disappeared into the crowd.

No one else seemed to notice what was going on with the young woman, or they just didn't care what was happening as long as it wasn't happening to them or someone they knew. In many clubs people will stop to watch the drama, but won't do or say anything to stop it. Either they're scared or they just don't want the hassle of getting involved. So it's important in this kind of environment to make sure that you have someone you trust watching your back.

Over the years managing night clubs, I've noticed that once you're inside there is no real security around. Most clubs concentrate their security by the entrance, exits, V.I.P, sections, and the cashier's window. There's usually not much security near the bar, restrooms, or dance floors—and that's where a lot of the drama starts. Security will come if someone calls them, but by then it may be too late to provide any help.

Another time, I was managing a club on Delware Avenue in Philadelphia when one of the guys from security waved me over to where he was standing with two black women. They looked to be in their late twenties and very drunk, and possibly high as well. They were dressed in tight blouses, mini-skirts, and high heels. One of the women looked dazed and had been crying her eyes out. We moved to an area of the club where it wasn't so loud, and I asked security what was going on. He told me that the woman who was crying said she had been raped in the back of the club.

The owner arrived and whisked us off to the cashier's booth, where it was a little quieter, although quite crowded. By the time we got the women settled on the room's only two chairs, the woman who had been crying looked out of it and in no condition to talk. Her cousin told us they had been at the bar drinking when four or five black men came over and started talking to them and buying them drinks. After a while, they asked if the women wanted to smoke some weed. They seemed so nice, the cousin said, that they agreed. She even had her eye on one and wanted to get his number before they left the club.

They went to the back of the club to smoke. After awhile other men joined them. They started dancing with various men and got separated. When she looked around for her cousin, she didn't see her and then she had problems of her own to contend with. The guy she was dancing with started feeling her up. At first she didn't mind, then he tried to slip his hands under her blouse and skirts. When she tried to walk away and was blocked by the other men, she got mad and started pushing and screaming.

Finally she broke away. She was furious with her cousin for not watching her back, but her temper disappeared when she found her cousin crumpled on the back steps, her head in her lap. Her cousin flinched when she touched her arm and for a few minutes just stared into space. Eventually her cousin let her take her hand and they walked over to where the security guy was standing. She told them that her cousin had been raped by some guys while she was on the dance floor.

The women couldn't identify the guys—they were all dressed in throwback jerseys, leather jackets, and jeans and wore baseball caps. The dumbass security guy even asked the woman how she knew then that there was more than one guy. She looked him straight in the face and said, "because the second guy's dick was bigger, asshole."

After she told us what had happened, I was surprised that no one said anything about calling the police or getting her to a hospital. The owner of the night club took the two women to his office. I assumed they were going to wait there until the police arrived. After the club closed for the night I found out that the woman who had been raped didn't want to wait for the police; she just wanted to go home. The owner gave her some money for her troubles, as if having complete strangers shove their fingers and dicks into her pussy was a minor irritation, and called them a taxi.

Had the police been called, they would have written up a report of the incident. Not only would the owner's insurance have gone up, but there was a real possibility that the club would be forced to close. This wasn't the only time something like this had happened in that club.

Only 32 percent of all rapes and sexual assaults are reported to the police. Of those cases actually brought to trial, 98 percent of the defendants get off scot free. Many women weigh the embarrassment and exposure a trial will inevitably bring and decide it's not worth it.

Years later while doing research on black men, I realized that different groups of black men were going around to different night clubs, looking for vulnerable women to have sex with, willingly or unwillingly. I call these men fiends because they are like hyenas. They run in packs and are very aggressive, out to scare their victims and wear down their resistance until they stop fighting. They target noisy clubs with dark corners and women who are alone. The fewer people she's with the easier it is to try their attack. They'll also single out women who are drunk or high on weed or pills.

Once they spot a victim, they'll meet and greet her with smiles and jokes. They'll offer to buy her drinks, knowing the drunker she is the harder it will be for her to put up a fight. They might talk her into smoking some weed to break her resistance even further. Then they'll herd her to a corner in the club where it's darkest and loudest. One of the pack asks her to dance and immediately starts feeling her up and grinding. If she's okay with the grinding and touching, then the rest of the hyenas move in. They crowd around so no one outside can see what they're doing and she can't get away.

Just because something happens to someone else doesn't mean it can't happen to you. There's nothing wrong with going out to night clubs. But you do need to be aware of what goes on in some clubs so you won't become a fiend's prey.

Signs of a Dangerous Night Club

1. No security around the restroom areas.
2. No separate restrooms for men and women.
3. No security near the dance floor or bar.
4. The club's security staff doesn't search everyone.
5. The club is so dark you can barely see who's next to you, and you can't see the dance floor and the back of the club when you enter the club.
6. No security inside the club.

Signs of a Safe Night Club

1. Separate restrooms for men and women.
2. Security near the restroom areas.
3. Security near or around the dance floor.
4. Security that searches everyone, even the V.I.P. guests (but not necessarily musicians, entertainers, or professional athletes who often travel with their own professional security guards)
5. Interior that is not pitch black and you can see what's going on.
6. Security inside the club.

Remember, you need always to be conscious of what's going on around you and have someone to watch your back. Like a designated driver, that someone won't drink, or won't drink much. I cannot emphasize enough the importance of having someone in your group or crew who is not drinking or cuts off after one. When you're intoxicated even just a little, you can easily be caught off guard. All it takes is a split second for someone to put something in your drink without you even noticing, like Rohypnol (roh-hip-nol).

You don't have to be drinking liquor to be slipped a date-rape drug. It can be just as undetectable in a ginger ale or cola. So never, ever take a drink from anyone. Get your own drink at the bar and watch your drink being mixed and made. Always keep your eyes on your drink. When you go out to dance, have someone in your group or crew watch the drinks. Never leave your drink without someone watching it.

Rohypnol is the trade name for flunitrazepam (floo-neye-traz- uh-pam). It is also known on the street and in night clubs as La Rochas, R-2, Rib, Roach, Roach-2, Circles, Lunch Money, Forget Oill, Mexican Valium, Roches, Mind Eraser, Roofies, Roopies, Poor Man's Quaalude, Rope, Rophies, Ruffles, and Whities.

Two other date-rape drugs have replaced Rohypnol in some parts of the United States: Clonazepam (which is marketed as Klonopin in the U.S. and Rivotril in Mexico) and Alprazolam (marketed as Xanax). Also commonly used date-rape drugs are GHB, which is short for gamma hydroxybutyric (gam-muh heye-drox-ee-byoo-tur-ick) acid. GBH is also known as: Bedtime Scoop, G, Gamma 10, Cherry Meth, Easy Lay, Energy Drink, Georgia Home Boy, G-Juice, PM, Salt Water, Gook, Goop, Soap, Liquid E, Liquid X, Liquid Ecstasy, Great Hormones, Vita-G, Grievous Bodily Harm, and Somatomax. The last but not the least of the date-rape drugs that are commonly used in parties and night clubs is Ketamine (keet-uh-meen), also known as Super Acid, Black Hole, Purple Special K, Bump, Cat Valium, K, Green, Jet, Kit Kat, Psychedelic Heroin, and K-Hole.

Information about date-rape drugs—the names, what they look or smell like, how they taste—should help you to protect yourself better and those who are with you when you go out partying.

If you are given Rohypnol, the effects can be felt within half an hour and can last for several hours. You will look and act as if you are drunk and you'll have trouble standing. Walking on your own is out of the question. Your speech will be slurred. You might pass out and not wake up for hours. These date-rape drugs affect women worse than others.

Rohypnol can cause the following problems:

1. Difficulty with motor movements.
2. Muscle relaxation or loss of muscle control.
3. Drunken feeling.
4. Loss of memory about what happened while drugged.
5. Nausea.
6. Speech difficulties.
7. Problems with vision.
8. Dizziness, sleepiness, and confusion.
9. Lowered blood pressure.
10. Stomach problems.
11. Death.

If you are given GHB, the effects can be felt within fifteen minutes and can last three to four hours. GHB is very potent and just a small amount can have a big effect on your body. You can easily overdose on GHB. That's why it's important that you always watch your drinks and who gives you an open drink (one not in a can or bottle). If someone puts too much GHB in your drink, you can be in real trouble. Most GHB is made by people in their home labs.

GHB can have the following effects:

1. Loss of consciousness and blackouts.
2. Relaxation, drowsiness.
3. Seizures and dizziness.

4. Loss of memory about what happened while you were drugged.
5. Tremors, sweating, vomiting, and nausea.
6. Lowered heart rate.
7. Induces dream-like state.
8. Coma and death.

If you are given Ketamine, the effects are also fast acting. While you are under this drug, you might be aware of what is happening to you, but you will be unable to move or resist anyone who is assaulting you. Later you might not remember what happened while you were drugged.

Ketamine can cause the following problems.

1. Loss of the sense of time and identity.
2. Distorted perceptions of sights and sounds.
3. Dream-like feelings.
4. Out-of-body sensations and experiences.
5. Feeling out of control.
6. Aggressive or violent behavior.
7. Impaired motor function.
8. Convulsions, numbness,
9. Depression.
10. Vomiting.
11. Breathing difficulties.
12. Impaired memory.
13. Slurred speech.
14. High blood pressure.
15. Loss of coordination.

You should know what these drugs look like so you will recognize them when you are out partying or clubbing.

Rohypnol comes in small pills that dissolve in liquids. The pills are usually round and white, although sometimes they come in oval form and are green-gray in color. When slipped into a drink, a dye in the pills makes clear liquids turn bright blue and a dark drink turn cloudy. This color change will be hard to notice in a dark room or area of the club or in dark drinks like Long Island Ice Tea, Hennessy, dark beer, or cola.

There are also Rohypnol pills with no dye in them that are still being sold and are available to those who want them. The pills can be ground up into a powder, which makes them easier to dissolve in your drink.

GHB comes in a few forms: small pills, a liquid with no color and no odor, and a white powder. GHB has a slightly salty taste. If mixed with a sweet drink, such as fruit juice, the sweetness can mask the salty taste.

Last but not least, Ketamine comes as a liquid and a white powder.

These drugs are very powerful and very dangerous. Many have no color, no smell, and no taste so you won't be able to tell if you are being drugged by a stranger or by someone you know and thought you could trust. Never forget that fiends wear many faces with smiles on them. It's not like the movies, where you can tell the good guys from the bad guys simply by looking at their faces.

Taking these drugs can damage the neurons in your brain, impair your judgment, your memory, your senses, and your coordination. Just because your girlfriend said she took one and it made her feel sexy and high, it doesn't mean that it will have the same effect on you. Seeing a girlfriend dancing, laughing, and partying hard after taking one is no reason for you to follow suit. The drug might kill you the very first time you try it or after using it a hundred times. So why take the chance? Your life is not like a PlayStation or Xbox game where you can hit restart when you've been killed. Once you're dead, you're dead. There are no second chances.

If someone gives you one of these drugs for fun or to party, they can cause you to go into a coma or even die if the dosage is too high or they are mixed with alcohol. They make rape easy and erase the memory. Never think it can't happen to you or someone you love and care about. It can happen to anyone. It happens to black women more than anyone else, and it's least reported to the police by black women because of shame or embarrassment. There's no reason to feel ashamed or embarrassed. It's the fiends who should feel the shame for the evil things they did.

Don't be fooled and watch only men. Date-rape drugs can be given to you by females also. You can't drop your guard because there are only women around you. Trust no one that you don't really know. Just because you've seen her or him around and know the families, you cannot assume you know the person. Now-a-days, men use women to set other women up for rapes, robberies, or assaults. These are some crazy times we're living in and you need to take care in where you go and with whom.

Another story I was told by a female friend illustrates how serious the situation can become when date-rape drugs are involved. Another female friend of ours was given a date-rape drug by a black man that she was dating and really liked. It turns out that he was setting her up to run a train on her. The night of the gang rape he gave her a drink laced with a date-rape drug. He and his friends took turns raping her. To make matters worse, they videotaped the whole gang rape and sold the copies.

Our friend was so ashamed and embarrassed that she ended up having a nervous breakdown and never recovered from the rape. She refused to report the gang rape because she thought it was her fault. Even though she had been tricked into the gang rape, she had willingly been having sex with the guy who set her up.

Alcohol can also be used as a date-rape drug. Anything that affects your judgment and behavior can put you at risk for unwanted or unsafe sexual activity. Alcohol is one such drug and is the drug most commonly used to help commit sexual assault.

When you're under a drug's influence, you are less able to sense danger. A 2007 University of Washington study found that both men and women tend to be more open to having unprotected sex when they drink moderate amounts of alcohol than when they're sober.

"As you become more intoxicated, you have trouble processing as much information from the environment. It's called *alcohol myopia*." If you've been drinking and both of you are hot and ready to have sex, the last thing on your mind is whether he has a condom or not.

What Happens When You Drink Too Much Alcohol

1. It's harder to say "no" to sexual advances.
2. It's harder to think clearly.
3. It's harder to set limits on what you want to do and what you don't want to do sexually.
4. It's harder to fight back if you are being sexually assaulted.
5. It's harder to tell when a situation is turning dangerous.
6. It's possible to blackout and have no memory of what happened to you.

The club and party drug Ecstasy (MDMA) has also been used by fiends to commit sexual assault. It can be slipped into your drink like any other date-rape drug without your knowledge. If you willingly take ecstasy, thinking it will make you feel more sexy and wonderful, you need to know that it increases the risk of being raped. Ecstasy can make you feel "lovey-dovey" toward others. It also can lower your ability to refuse sexual advances.

Any intoxication—whether from alcohol or weed or a date-rape drug—lowers your awareness, makes you drop your guard, and increases your desire for sexual contact, even if sober you didn't want it. Your body talks for you when your guard is down. Over the years black men have told me that's why they don't mind buying a woman drinks all night. They hope to knock her guard down so they can get what they want even if she didn't initially want it.

Things to Do When You Go Out Clubbing or Partying

1. Never, ever let anyone bring you a drink.
2. Don't order drinks from the wait staff. Why? While they're on their way to your table, someone can easily distract them and slip a date-rape drug into your drink, especially when the club is crowded.
3. Get your own drink or have someone from your group or crew go to the bar to get everyone drinks. Better yet, order a closed bottle and have it opened in front of you.
4. Keep your drink with you at all times, even when you go to the restroom.
5. Never, ever share someone's drink. Go get your own drink.
6. If someone offers to buy you a drink or get one from the bar, go to the bar with him and watch your drink being made and always carry it yourself.
7. Never, ever drink from punch bowls or other common, open containers. They might have date-rape drugs in them.
8. Always have a non-drinking family member or friend with you to watch your back and what' going on around you.
9. If you realize you left your drink unattended, throw it away and get another. It's not worth the risk to drink it. You can't be sure that someone hasn't slipped something into it. Spend the extra few dollars to be safe and buy another drink.
10. If you feel drunk and have had only one alcoholic drink or only soda, or if you feel the effects of the alcohol are stronger than usual, seek help from security right away.

It's often hard to tell when you've been drugged or assaulted. Most victims of an assault or rape after being given a date-rape drug don't remember anything. Sometimes the victim might not be aware that they have been attacked until six to twelve hours after the crime. These drugs also leave the body very quickly. If, for instance, you were drugged with one of these date-rape drugs and sexually assaulted or raped, you might not realize it and get up to urinate, shower or bathe, wash your hands, or brush your teeth. Any of these things will wash away the evidence of a sexual assault or rape and date-rape drugs.

Signs That You Might Have Been Drugged

1. You wake up feeling disoriented, with a very bad hangover.
2. You have no memory of how you got where you are or who brought you there.
3. You feel drunk and don't remember drinking any alcohol or you think the effect of the alcohol has been stronger than usual.
4. After waking up, you remember having a drink, but can't remember anything after that.
5. You wake and find that your clothes are torn, not on right, or items are missing.
6. You wake up feeling you have had sex, but can't remember it.

If you have any of these feelings after a night clubbing or partying, call 911 and get medical treatment right away. Have a family member or trusted friend take you to a hospital emergency room. Don't urinate, douche, take a bath or shower, brush your teeth, wash your hands, change your clothes, or drink or eat anything before you go to the hospital. You might destroy the evidence of the rape. The hospital will use a rape kit to collect evidence.

When you get to the hospital, call the police again to let them where you are and what exactly you remember. Always be honest about everything you did and don't forget to include smoking marijuana or drinking alcohol. Whatever you did doesn't justify being raped.

Be sure to ask the hospital to take a urine sample that can be used to test for date-rape drugs. Rohypnol stays in your body for several hours and can be detected in the urine up to seventy-two hours after taking it. GHB leaves the body in twelve hours. Also, don't clean up where you think the assault might have occurred. There could be evidence left behind—on drinking glasses, bed sheets, or blankets.

Warning to Black Women Who Dance at Strip Clubs for a Living

Women who work in strip clubs must be extra careful and vigilant. Dancers must leave their drinks when they perform and can't keep an eye on them. Sometimes a dancer needs a drink or two or three to get through the day or night. And men go to strip clubs to be aroused and titillated, with sex on their minds.

Never, ever take a drink from someone at the strip clubs where you are working, and never, ever drink from someone else's glass because they could have put a roofie in their own drink to fake you out. A fiend will also put a date-rape drug at the bottom of the glass with an ice cube hiding it and have you watch him pour you a drink. To be on the safe side, take drinks from no one but the bartender.

A fiend told me a revealing story. He and his partner were at a strip club one night and had a sexy young woman dancing for them. They were buying her drinks, and his partner wanted to have sex with her in the Champagne Room. She told him that she didn't have sex for money, and that she had a boyfriend. He could tell that his partner was upset and then noticed his partner pouring something into her drink.

After she drank it and took a few hits from the blunt his partner had laced with Ecstasy, she could hardly stand while she was trying to dance for them and kept nodding off when she sat down. His partner started feeling her up and she no longer put up any resistance.

Then his partner suggested that they take her to his place. They helped her stand up and walked her down the steps of the strip club.

The security guard paid no attention. Seeing men leaving with dancers was really nothing new in that business.

Once they were outside, another dancer came rushing out the door, screaming at them. Where were they going with her girlfriend? His partner turned on her like he wanted to shoot her. She must have sensed the danger because she rushed back into the strip club, yelling that she was going to call the police.

His partner hurriedly put the drugged dancer in his truck. By now she was out cold with her legs wide open on the back seat. Then his partner jumped in the front seat and took off.

When I asked him why he didn't go along, he admitted that he didn't feel right about this one—implying that they had done this sick shit before. He saw his partner a few days later and was told that he had called some more friends to come over and have their way with her. The pack of them even took pictures of the action.

Cocaine is another major danger for black women who have just returned to the partying and clubbing scene after getting separated or divorced. Without any warning, cocaine can cause a fatal reaction at any time in any kind of user—not just heavy users, but light, so- called recreational users who smoke, snort, or drink it at weekend parties and at clubs. One of these recreational users, a twenty-one- year-old black woman from Ft. Lauderdale, Florida, went to a house party, drank some alcohol, snorted some cocaine, and then told her girlfriends that she needed to lie down. She wasn't feeling so good, she said; she must have eaten something that didn't agree with her. A little while later she had a violent seizure. An ambulance was called, but she died before it arrived.

She had used cocaine on previous occasions as a party and clubbing drug. For some reason or another, her body without any warning had suddenly developed an intolerance for the drug. Drug-abuse experts warn that there is no way of predicting who will die from cocaine use. It could be a regular user or a first-time user. Why take the chance? Cocaine is a poison. When used pharmaceutically in hospitals, it comes in bottles with the familiar poison warning, a skull and crossbones, on the label.

Some date-rape drugs are legal when used for medical purposes. But that doesn't mean that they are safe. These drugs are very powerful and can hurt you. They should be used only under a doctor's care and order. Rohypnol is not legal in the United States, although it is prescribed in Europe and Mexico for sleep problems and with anesthesia before surgery. Rohypnol is brought into the United States illegally. Ketamine, however, is legal for use as an anesthetic for humans and animals, but is mostly used on animals. Veterinary clinics are frequently robbed for their Ketamine supplies. If you suspect that you have been a victim of any of these date- rape drugs, get counseling and treatment right away. Feelings of shame, guilt, fear, and shock are normal after a trauma like this. A counselor can help you work through these emotions so you can begin the healing process. Calling a crisis center or hotline is a good place to start. One national hotline is the National Sexual Assault Hotline at 800-656-HOPE.

Important Things to Remember When You Go Out Clubbing

1. Never let yourself get separated from the friends or family members you came to the club with.
2. Always know where your family or friends are in the club.
3. Never go to the restroom by yourself. At least have someone wait outside, by the door, until you come out.
4. Don't go in dark places of the club by yourself.
5. Don't let a man you've just met take you to a dark part of the club or party without someone in your group knowing where you are.
6. Don't take drinks from anyone unless you were there when the drink was made and never take your eyes off your drink.

7. Always have someone in your group watch your drink when you dance. Better yet, finish your drink before you go dancing.
8. Check where security is just in case you need them.
9. Keep some kind of mace or pepper spray in your handbag or pocketbook. It's best to have something for protection, even if you never have to use it.

Black women, in these wild and crazy times, you have to be very careful about the people you let bring you or give you a drink—even someone you know from work or from around the neighborhood. You can think they're good people, but you really don't know until you have some dealings with them or have seen how they treat others. It's a known fact that the majority of violent crimes against women are committed by someone they know or thought they knew. You need to be conscious of what's going on around you while you are out there clubbing and partying.

Chapter 10

Love Is Blind

What I Wish for All Black Women

Happiness deep down within your heart and soul because
you are strong. You know it and I know it. I believe in you.
I always have and I always will. I hope and pray that life gets better
for you. If it's not getting better, be strong and keep your faith in God
always.

Have courage. Refuse to be defeated. A lot of times
things don't go as we hoped and planned, but with effort, patience
and persistence, things will come your way.
Life will open up for you.

I wish for you serenity with each sunrise, success in
each facet of your life, close and caring family and friends. Love
that's never ending for you. Special memories of all the yesterdays
that mean and meant so much to you. Bright todays with so much to
be thankful for. A path that leads to beautiful tomorrows.
Dreams that do their very best to come true, but most of all I
wish for you to appreciate
all the wonderful things about yourself.

One in six women in the United States will be assaulted by their intimate partner over her lifetime. That's almost 300,000 rapes or sexual assaults a year. The numbers are slightly higher for black women and women of color (18.8% versus 17.6%). The vulnerable ages are between 18 and 34 with girls 16 to 19 four times more likely to be raped or sexually assaulted.

The violence starts early, as black girls begin dating young, not thinking about marriage, only about hooking up with a guy. But he begins acting as if he's already her husband, putting his hands on her, wanting to know where she's going and who's she's going with, or who's she's talking to on the phone.

These young black boys watch their fathers hit their mothers, their uncles beat their aunts. Over time they come to think this behavior is normal. In a twisted way, they may even believe that "disciplining" a wife or girlfriend is a man's right, if not his duty, and part of loving. Once a young black man reaches a certain age, it's harder to get him to listen to advice, to understand that violence toward women is not acceptable and never justified. He's often grown up surrounded by domestic violence and takes it for granted.

When I was about ten, my aunts and uncles came to visit. Then my mother went out with them to a night club. She didn't get in until late that night. Sounds of footsteps on the stairs and angry voices woke me up. Curious, I crept to the door and listened. My father was shouting at my mother. Where had she been? Why was she getting home so late?

I snuck out of my room and tiptoed to the living-room door. I watched my father hit my mother across the face with my two aunts sitting right there. He hissed something at her and stalked out of the room without noticing me. Appalled, my aunts rushed to my mother's side to comfort her. They insisted on calling my uncles to tell them what my father had done. My mother begged them not to—more than anything, she seemed embarrassed that her husband had hit her in front of her sisters. My aunts called my uncles anyway.

I went back to bed, but a little while later angry voices again woke me up. My two big uncles were shouting at my farther, warning him never to put his hands on their sister again. I don't remember exactly what was said; I just remember my father didn't say a word. After that, I never saw my father hit my mother. But who know what happened behind closed doors?

Twenty-four percent of all murders take place in the home, and most of the victims are women who die at the hands of men who claim to love them. How can you ever hurt a woman—a wife or a girlfriend—that you say you love? It's a lie. A man who claims to love you will never hurt you. Don't believe a word a black man tells you if he beats you or abuses you verbally. Abuse is abuse—whether it's with his hands or his words, whether it's physical, psychological, or emotional.

In many relationships, the various forms of abuse work in concert and the abuse escalates over time. Almost half (48.4%) of the women in serious relationships experience psychological manipulation and 4 in 10 suffer coercive control. Abuse takes place across all economic and educational levels. Financial security and academic or professional credentials don't guarantee escape. The woman who is the family's primary breadwinner or makes more than her partner is more at risk than a woman who doesn't work.

Never take it for granted that you are safe from abuse. The best precaution is to be aware of the characteristics of an abusive personality and watch carefully for them when you are starting a new relationship.

Warning Signs of an Abusive Personality

1. He is rigid; it's his way or the highway. His needs and wants always take priority over yours.
2. He has violent mood swings: One minute he's real nice and sweet; the next he's saying mean, nasty, and crazy things to you.

3. He criticizes you—how you dress, your makeup, the way you talk or laugh.
4. He dislikes your friends and doesn't get along with your family.
5. He gets mad when you talk to other men, even long-time friends.
6. He wants you to be available all the time and gets annoyed when you are not at his beck and call.
7. He constantly keeps track of where you are and who's with you.
8. He'll threaten to hurt you if he thinks you're lying to him. (The operative word here is "thinks"; he might not believe your denials even when you are telling the truth.)
9. He'll press you to make out or have sex even when you are not in the mood.
10. He'll demand you take part in sexual acts that make you uncomfortable.

As a black woman, you must take these warning signs very seriously. You get no second chances. Once you discover your man might be abusive, forget about hurting his feelings. Forget him. It's about your life. If he doesn't understand what makes you happy and care that you are happy, then you don't need him in your life.

All my life I've watched abuse—verbal and physical—being meted out to black women by black men. When I was in my twenties, I witnessed a tragic illustration of just how deadly abuse can turn. The story involves friend—a basketball player who was 6'3" and weighed anywhere between 225 and 240 pounds—and his girlfriend, a beautiful, loving black woman.

In their twenties the two of them had fallen in love and had a daughter together. In the beginning everything was beautiful and loving. He talked about her more than I had ever heard him talk about any woman. But over time he became obsessed with her:

Where was she? Why didn't she answer the phone? Why hadn't she returned his call? What was she doing?

I paid no attention to the warning signs that his obsession had become unhealthy, if not dangerous. I'd never seen him like this; he'd always had a lot of women in and out of his life. Because he was a basketball star and in the city league, women were always after him.

When a college basketball scholarship didn't come through, he got into selling drugs. Then he met her. I never knew how they met, but from then on she was all he talked about. One day, hanging out, he told me she was a Philadelphia police officer, assigned to the area where his crew was selling drugs, and was passing along intelligence from the drug squad.

At first I don't think she knew he was dealing. By the time she found out, it was too late; she was in love with him. Eventually it got to her—that the father of her baby and the man she loved was selling drugs.

When she told him that she couldn't be with him if he kept selling drugs, he didn't want to hear it. He went ballistic. Not only was she refusing to feed him information, she had the nerve to threaten to leave him. Who did she think she was? She was his baby's mother and should do whatever he told her to do. So what if she was a police officer? He didn't care. He became so emotionally, verbally, and physically abusive, she took out a restraining order against him.

A few weeks later, watching the news, I was stunned. She had been murdered in her apartment with her own gun. Every police officer in the city was looking for my friend. They conducted a citywide manhunt for him. I never imagined that he would kill that beautiful, kind, caring woman, the mother of his child, and the woman he claimed to love.

There is a lesson here. As a black woman, never underestimate where a "little" abuse—attempts to control, possessiveness, the occasional slap—can lead. If a man has the nerve to curse you out or hit you, he may develop the nerve to kill you.

My friend was obsessive—he wanted to be in control of every aspect of his woman's life. When he lost that control, he killed her. But obsession is not the only dangerous characteristic of abusive men. They can be insanely jealous and possessive. From the day my cousin met his wife, he was possessive about her. He viewed her as his property. When she no longer wanted to be with him and started talking about divorce, he went crazy. If he couldn't have her, nobody else would either. He tried everything he could think of to keep her from filing for divorce.

When she left the state for North Carolina to get away from him, he followed. He went to her house where she lived with her son (not his), still determined to convince her to give him another chance. She refused and he beat her to death. After he murdered her, he took her car and her little son to the woods somewhere in North Carolina. He walked the little boy into the woods and killed him too. The police caught him a few days later, still driving her car, and charged him with two counts of murder.

Many black men who hurt or kill their wives don't care about getting caught. The rage they feel toward the one they claim to love blinds them. If they're not going to have her, they'll make sure no one else does or wants to. So when your husband or boyfriend tells you that he will kill you, believe him. Don't fool yourself and think that he loves you too much to hurt you. Never underestimate any man when he says he wants to hurt you.

My cousin's wife had done all she could to break away—divorced him, moved away. With a man like this, your only escape is to avoid getting entangled with him in the first place. If you are already involved, it's time to cut out if you know it's over and he keeps after you, promising anything and everything to keep you in his life.

An abusive man doesn't have to kill you to destroy your life. He can ruin it simply by taking over, controlling every minute of your day. First he might object to your friends. Then he picks a quarrel with your relatives, and they stop visiting. Soon you are isolated—

cut off from any source of support or help and totally dependent on him.

Although one in six black women are assaulted or abused, most (68%) don't report the crime to the police—often because they blame themselves. An abusive black man victimizes his woman emotionally, not just physically. He'll attack with words that rip apart your self-esteem. "You're lucky I stay with you. No one else would. You're so fat, so ugly, so stupid." He will complain that you are a failure as a woman—you can't even get supper on the table on time, do the laundry properly, or service him in bed the way he likes. (Ninety percent of the time victims of physical abuse or sexual assault experience psychological or emotional abuse as well).

After months of hearing that you're worthless, you may come to believe it and be grateful that he's sticking around. The psychological bond is so deep, so complex, in an abusive relationship that the women take as gospel the negative comments, think they've earned the smacks. It's no wonder the women ends up blaming herself. She's heard over and over that all the problems in his life are her fault. He may even play on her sympathies. If he hits her, he'll apologize and sometimes sob that he cannot lose her. He does what he does because he loves her so much. He will try to make up with flowers, gifts, jewelry and promise never to hit her again—which is a lie. He will hit her again, have no doubt about that.

No one needs this kind of love from anyone. No matter what a man is giving you and doing for you, no matter how scared you are of being alone, an abusive man will ruin your life and maybe your children's lives.

Warning Signs That You Are Already in an Abusive Relationship

1. You feel as if he wants to own you, that you are his property.

2. You are constantly bombarded with insults in public as well as in private and called "bitch," "cunt," "dummy" or similar labels.
3. You get blamed for everything that's wrong in his life and the relationship.
4. You have to dress to please him; if he doesn't like what you're wearing, you must change.
5. You avoid talking to other men, even friends, because he gets mad and accuses you of flirting or worse.
6. You think he might be going through your pocketbook and checking your cell phone to see the people you've called and who have called you.
7. You can't see your friends much anymore because he dislikes them, and you seldom visit your family because he doesn't get along with them.
8. You have to account for every penny you spend and he thinks nothing of taking credit cards out in your name or of keeping you away from your job, even forcing you to quit.
9. You are frightened that he will take your children away if you leave him—he holds the threat over you constantly.
10. You never know when he's going to fly off the handle over some minor thing and yell at you or hit you.

As a black woman, you have the right to tell any man you no longer want him in your life if all he does is bring you down. There is power in your words; use them when you're not happy in your marriage or relationship.

Don't let anyone abuse you and stay silent. Draw on the power of your words to express yourself. He needs to know exactly how you feel about what he has done to you. If he won't listen, get out. An abusive partner can damage not only you, but your children. Children ape their parents' behavior. They watch their parents and absorb what they see. Abuse is not something you want repeated in the next generation. That reason alone should be enough for you to want positive men in your life.

Just because you love someone, it doesn't mean that you are meant to be together. You may love a man with all your heart, but he may be no good for you. Too much love is bad love when it becomes an obsession. There are a lot of good, loving, caring black men out there waiting for you.

A lot of times those who are a part of our lives at one point are just stepping stones to the person we are meant to be with. A real man who really cares about you will see the best in you and lift you up when you need it most. Even when you stop believing in yourself, he still believes in you.

If you've managed to escape from an abusive relationship, take one day at a time. Don't look back and grieve over what has happened in the past. There's nothing you can do to change that. But you must learn from that past experience, not beat yourself up over it.

The key to healing is to forgive—mostly yourself, but him as well. If you continue to hate him, you waste emotional capital; he's still in your thoughts and still has power over your emotions, whether you admit it or not. So forgive—but never forget. You don't want to make the same mistake again. Before you can move on you have to L.I.G.— Let It Go. You must let go of the pain and the hurt before you can find real love and happiness.

But not all abuse takes place within marriages or relationships between adults. In a troubling variant, the victims are young girls and teens who are just starting to date or looking for a guy to hook up with. Although a lot of date abuse comes in the form of coercive control or possessiveness, over 40 percent of girls under eighteen have been raped or sexually assaulted. Any girl between sixteen and nineteen is four times more likely than other women to be raped or assaulted.

Many experts say that the signs of date abuse don't always show up in black-and-blue bruises and many are hard to spot. Moreover, young girls struggling to handle emotional and physical intimacy for the first time in their lives may throw off confusing signals that can be mistaken for the warning signs of abuse. They may not even realize they are involved in an abusive relationship.

The statistics are alarming. One in three teenagers says she knows a friend who has been beaten, hit, slapped, kicked, or choked by her boyfriend. Young black girls, you must understand that date violence is a form of oppression; that it is not right. You shouldn't have to deal with it growing up, but you do. There are signs that you can pick up on that will warn you that your relationship may be not all it promised to be.

Warning Signs for Teens That They Might Be Getting Into or Involved in an Abusive Relationship

1. You no longer eat the way you used to.
2. You feel sad. For no obvious reason, you break down crying or get depressed.
3. You've changed the kind of clothes you wear, either to suit your boyfriend or to hide parts of your body.
4. You retreat to your room and don't speak to anyone when you come home although you used to watch television together or help in the kitchen with dinner.
5. You think the guy is great, but wish you could hang with your girlfriends the way you used to do.
6. You're concerned about school—your grades are dropping, but your boyfriend just laughs off the worries.
7. You find your self-confidence slipping and more and more often have to fake assurance.
8. You like having the guy—he's cool and adds to your status—but you are getting uncomfortable with his increasing demands.
9. You aren't enjoying the sex. It's sometimes rough and you don't like some of the things you're asked to do.

As a young black girl, you have the world and your whole life in front of you. You don't have to change because some guy tells you to. If you can't wait, or don't want to wait, to get married before you have sex, you should arm yourself with the facts. You should insist that your sexual partner wear a condom, but be aware that condoms don't always work or protect you from catching HIV or STDs. Young black boys or men will also trick you. They'll plot to get you pregnant by pretending to have a condom on or by taking it off during intercourse. Some will protest that they don't need to use a condom. "I'll pull out before I come" or "I'm only going to stick the head of my penis in your pussy." You can still get pregnant or catch HIV or an STD.

Moreover, many men don't know how to put on a condom for full protection. According to a 2012 Kinsey Institute study, men make one or two mistakes. They either forget to leave space for their semen to collect at the condom's tip, or if they do leave a little room, they fail to squeeze out the air. Both of these mistakes increase the risk of breakage. The proper technique for putting on a condom is to leave space at the tip and remove the air by squeezing the tip with a thumb and forefinger as the condom is rolled all the way to the base of the penis.

The decisions you are making now, as a young black girl, can shape your life or change it forever. Having a baby, for example, will not make the other problems you face go away.

In my city, a beautiful, intelligent black teenager was murdered by the father of the baby she was carrying. Why? He didn't want her to have the baby. He was over twenty-one, but she was only sixteen when she became pregnant. He was afraid of being charged with statutory rape. She went missing for weeks. Everyone was looking for her—from the police to members of the community. There was even a reward posted for any information about her.

The police found her battered body in the park, rolled up in a carpet. They arrested the man for murdering her and his unborn child. This monster was so cold that he even called a radio station to protest his innocence. So never, ever underestimate what a black boy or man can do. His youth or relatively young age won't protect you.

The best protection is to be informed and surround yourself with positive friends who support your goals and dreams and respect you and your feelings.

Black mothers also need to keep a watchful eye out—for their sons as well as their daughters. By age twelve, a quarter of all children are having sex, with the percentage rising to 59 between ages thirteen and sixteen. One in three teens have passed around nude photographs on their iPhones. Young black boys must be taught how to respect, protect, and love black girls. Young black girls need to know that there is a double standard at work. A young black man can have sex with twenty to thirty women, and he's looked up to by other men, even other women. Let a young black girl sleep around and she's labeled a whore, easy, slut, or loose and those labels can stick.

Warning Signs for Mothers of Young Black Daughters

1. She no longer eats and worries constantly about her weight even though you think she looks great.
2. She seems depressed and you can't figure out why.
3. She's wearing more makeup and you suspect she's trying to cover bruises.
4. She's dressing differently—either in provocative short skirts or outfits that hide her body.
5. She always wants to be in her room. She'll come into the house and not speak to anyone.
6. She no longer gets visits or phone calls from her girlfriends.
7. She's withdrawn from family activities (like cookouts).
8. She's moody and spends a lot of time in the bathroom.

9. She avoids being in the same room with your boyfriend or her stepfather.
10. She brings the screen-saver up on her computer whenever you come into her room.

These signs may not signal a daughter's involvement in an abusive relationship. She may simply be having difficulty handling a new relationship or one that is changing—particularly if it's her first serious involvement. Without prying or pressuring your daughter to share confidence, try to create situations where she can open up and then listen hard when she does. She's covering new ground and might find your experiences and advice helpful. She will definitely appreciate the support and concern.

Your antennae should go on alert, however, if your child tells you that someone has touched or harmed her physically or sexually, even if the explanation is garbled or confused.

It's a good idea to discourage your young daughters, sisters, and nieces from dressing like grown women. Provocative clothes on young girls can be an open invitation to sickos who prey on pretty young things. If you have the slightest suspicion, you might want to check their bags or pocketbooks for extra clothes and makeup to make sure they are not changing once they leave the house.

Pimps and sex traffickers prey on young black girls who are lonely and insecure and looking for some man or boy to show them attention. Once one of these fiends gets hold of an innocent, trusting teen, he will entrap her with promises and feigned affection. When she's completely under his spell, he will hold her hostage. He will abuse her physically and psychologically until she is too weak to fight back and too afraid to ask for help from a police officer who might be standing ten feet away. She's so broken in body and spirit that she doesn't even think about escaping from him.

A young black girl with low self-esteem or an unhappy home life is easily brainwashed. Once a fiend has her under control, he'll put her on the streets to make money to take care of them. In reality, all the money goes to him.

Pimps and other predators are masters at manipulation. It's imperative that you know the boys or men your daughter or young relations are dating. Fiends are known to dress and look like well-mannered college students. That's just a part of the games they play to get their hands on innocent young black girls. To make things worse, rap videos often portray pimps and pimping as something fun, which desensitizes young black girls to the actual dangers of life on the streets.

According to U.S. Department of Justice estimates, over 300,000 American children are at risk of being forced into prostitution. A lot of these girls are so brainwashed that when they are picked up by the police for vagrancy or soliciting, they refuse to give the real names of their pimps or to identify them. Without positive identification, the police have to let the pimps back on the street— where they can victimize more young black girls.

Domestic sex trafficking has nearly doubled since 2008. Sex predators use free Internet sites like Craigslist to sell sex with innocent young girls—and boys. There is little chance of being caught. According to Advanced Interactive Media Group figures, Craigslist earns approximately $36 million a year from its adult services postings. These ads feature barely dressed young females, bending over chairs or on a bed fondling their naked breasts. U.S. Department officials say sex trafficking in teenage girls and boys has worsened since drug dealers have gotten into the action. Exploiting young girls and boys, it turns out, is more profitable and less risky than selling drugs.

It's important to pay attention to what your daughter may be doing on her computer or iPad. There could be a predator in her room, and you wouldn't know until it's too late. Pimps nowadays use the web to groom and sell young girls. These fiends will talk to a teen for hours in a chat room and draw her out with fake sympathy. "I know what you must be going through. Your mom sounds a real bitch."

If you monitor her computer time, a daughter will probably accuse you of invading her privacy. That is a perfect opportunity to explain why you need to know about anyone she is chatting with on her computer. Tell her everything so she'll understand that these predators are dangerous and that you only want to protect her from harm. That fifteen-year-old boy she's been chatting to online might be a forty-year-old man trying to get her somewhere alone. She must be warned never to tell someone online where she goes to school or where she lives. A pimp or sexual predator can be anyone, someone she knows or doesn't know, a landlord, doctor, or government employee, a teenage boy at her school.

The underground sex industry makes it nearly impossible for law enforcement to combat the trafficking in young boys and girls without help from the parents or guardians. If you think something is wrong with the boys your daughter is chatting with online, call the police. We can't watch our children twenty-four hours a day. But we should at least know where they're going and who is going with them and what they are doing online.

Abuse can take many forms and doesn't spare any age group. The control can be so subtle that it's only gradually that you realize you have lost your sense of identity, that he's swallowed it up. At first the possessiveness, all that attention centered on you, may seem flattering—until your house or apartment begins to feel like a prison. Or, as we have seen, it can turn vicious, dangerous and deadly. Whatever form the abuse assumes, you don't deserve it. You owe it to yourself to protest—for yourself and for other black women who may feel, as you have, isolated and alone, with nowhere to turn. There's a beautiful world out there waiting for you—but you have to give yourself the chance to find it.

Statistics in this chapter were taken from numerous sources: the U.S. Bureau of Justice Statistics, the National Institute of Justice & Centers for Disease Control and Prevention: *Prevalence and Consequences of Violence Against Women Survey*; RAINN (Rape, Abuse, & Incest National Network; and National Coalition Against Domestic Violence.

Chapter 11

The Best Kept Secrets

Marriage should celebrate the unity of two unique individuals—that of a man and a woman. They join hands to travel the road of life, to give love openly and honestly. Marriage shouldn't be full of lies and deceit at the very beginning. If it is, then it's bound for unhappiness, drama, pain, and emptiness.

I was thirty-seven when I first encountered the strip club scene. One of my cousins, the owner of the record label where I was the studio manager, had a meeting scheduled one night at a gentlemen's club called Delilah's in Philadelphia. About eight of us piled into two SUVs. On the ride to Delilah's no one mentioned that we were going to a strip club. When we pulled up in front of the club, one of our studio people greeted the doorman, and I assumed he was a regular customer.

Once inside Delilah's I immediately understood why so many men got hooked on strip clubs. The place was nothing like I'd ever seen—more like an exclusive night club or fancy restaurant than the sleazy joint I imagined. The club served all kinds of food. Delilah's certainly wasn't what I was expecting.

Once the hostess seated us in the V.I.P. section, we were bum-rushed by all kinds of dancers—black, white, Latina, and Asian. One dancer asked if I wanted her to dance for me. Before I could answer, my cousin handed me a wad of twenties, and we were off for my lap dance. I asked how much a lap dance cost, having never been to a strip club or paid a woman to dance for me. She told me it was twenty dollars a lap dance. By the end of the night, I'd spent three or four hundred dollars on lap dances. I thought it was a waste of money. I could have used that money to pay some bills. But since it wasn't coming out of my pocket, I didn't think too much about it; I just had fun that night.

The way we ran the record label everything was a tax write-off. Almost all our business meetings were at nice restaurants or clubs. I found out later that Delilah's was the top strip club in Philadelphia and the tri-state area. Only men who had a lot of money to spend went to Delilah's. It cost twenty-five dollars just to get in the door.

After my experience at Delilah's, I thought that all strip clubs were like that. Months later, I found out how wrong that assumption was. I needed some extra money. My studio take wasn't covering the bills and I needed cash for a trip to California to be with my family. Out of nowhere, a friend asked if I would help him run a strip club he had just opened.

The strip club's hours were 6 p.m. to 4 a.m., Tuesday to Sunday. I worked the front door with another security man who searched everyone. I collected the money—five dollars per person. I was making anywhere from seventy-five to a hundred and fifty dollars a night, depending on the crowd.

The club was in West Philly, which was perfect for me. I lived just a few blocks away and could get a couple of hours sleep before I had to open the studio at ten the next morning. Even being from the neighborhood, I had never heard of a club around there.

The first night I was to show up for work, I went to the address my friend had given me. I had to look at the card twice to make sure I had the right address. The club was in an old three-story house, next to an abandoned building and what looked like an auto garage with a few abandoned or used cars and trucks in the lot. What have I agreed to? I was thinking.

I was just about to change my mind and roll when the front door opened. A black man who looked like a linebacker for a professional football team came out. He was every bit of 6'6" and 275 pounds. When I told him who I was, his face lit up and his hand went out. He said his name was Bear, and he was expecting me. Once inside, Bear gestured me upstairs where my hommie, the owner, was.

Upstairs the place looked like an after-hours dance club from back in the day. There was a small bar against the wall at the top of the stairs and the main room had about a dozen tables and chairs. Loveseats ringed the back and side walls, which were painted black, blue, and purple and decorated with posters of different rappers and R&B singers. In the back, a purple door led to the room where the strippers changed their outfits and a bathroom where a stripper could shower if she needed one before going home. There was a small stage in the front of the club about two feet high with a silver pole that ran from the middle of the stage to the ceiling and some track lights on the ceiling.

The place was nothing like Delilah's. If Delilah's was the top of the line, this place had to be the bottom, or close to it. Nor were the dancers anything like the dancers at Delilah's, who all could have passed for models. At this place the strippers came in all shapes and sizes. Some were sexy, but most were out of shape and squeezed into cheap outfits a couple sizes too small. To be honest, a lot of them looked a mess. I couldn't believe that black men would pay to have these strippers dance for them, let alone touch them.

Downstairs Bear searched almost everyone, except the men he knew. They would tip him some extra money either coming in or leaving the club. After a few nights I realized that only black men visited this club.

One night after working the door for about five hours, I had to use the restroom. After my bathroom break, I went to the bar to get something to drink. Once my eyes adjusted to the dark, I could see what was going on. Strippers were performing all kinds of sexual acts everywhere. The place looked like a live sex show, with a lot of one-on-one fucking and sucking going on right in front of everyone. There was no lap dancing to be seen.

When I got back downstairs, I asked Bear if it was like that every night upstairs. Almost every night, Bear said, but it's craziest on Fridays and Saturdays. I worked there for almost five months. It certainly wasn't a gentlemen's club—far from it. But I learned a great deal about black men in those five months. Working there opened my eyes to another myth.

I had always thought you weren't allowed to touch the dancers or strippers, but they could touch you if they wanted to. At this club, the men could touch whenever, wherever, and whomever they wanted.

There was even a fee scale. For twenty bucks, a guy could fondle a stripper's breast or play between her legs; oral sex cost thirty to fifty dollars; and intercourse, seventy-five to a hundred. A lot of the strippers had regular customers that they charged less, but if a customer was a baller or drug dealer, they'd charge more. They knew that ballers and drug dealers had it to spend.

The vast majority of men who came through the doors were drug dealers or hustlers. It was easy spot them from the way they dressed and the vehicles they drove. Besides, working men don't flash rolls of twenties, fifties, and hundreds as if they were nothing.

Most of the strippers were doing more than just dancing. Many left with the black men who were their customers or had them wait outside until the club closed. In my mind, they went from strippers to hookers. They just didn't stand on street corners. I don't judge anyone—or what a woman does to survive. I'm just telling it like it is.

The black men who came to the club often had wives and girlfriends and children at home. The strippers themselves provided the information. After we closed, we would sit around while everyone counted the money they'd made that night. The strippers would gossip about their customers—what the men wanted from them. Some of the men even offered to buy them cars or set them up with regular money or nice apartments if they would stop stripping. Others would ask for their phone numbers so they could call anytime they wanted. These customers would tell the stripper about their wives or girlfriends, about how they won't do sexual things for them. That was the excuse they gave for coming to a strip club.

I could only handle five months of working at the club. It just wasn't my thing, only something I did to make some extra money. While I was working for the strip club, strippers would ask me to drive them to private parties or bachelor parties to provide security. Without security, the strippers could run into trouble collecting their money or the party could get out of hand. I thought private parties and bachelor parties would be better than standing in the hallway of the strip club with just a heater to keep warm. Boy was I wrong.

Bachelor parties were definitely not what I expected. I had never had a bachelor party and hadn't realized the wild and crazy things that went on at them.

For over fifty years bachelor parties have remained the best-kept secret among black men, even better kept than what really goes on in strip clubs. At the strip clubs, the strippers and dancers use dance as a cover for sex for sale. At bachelor parties sex is part of the invitation.

Before I got married, my brother, who was my best man, and other male relatives were very upset that I didn't want to have a bachelor party. Most of the friends or relatives who were disappointed were married or in so-called serious relationships.

Even months after the wedding, my brother was still bummed, protesting that he would have paid for the bachelor party. I told him he could give me the money instead as a wedding present. I never saw the money and never understood what the big deal was about bachelor parties until I started doing security for them.

The first bachelor party that I did security for was wild from the moment the strippers and dancers came into the room. The party was held in a big suite at a hotel by the airport. The suite smelled of liquor and weed. An X-rated movie was playing on the hotel channel and music from a boombox on a table.

Almost everyone had a drink or a blunt in their hands. The strippers and dancers went into the bedroom to change. A few minutes later they came out in their sexy outfits and got straight to work doing their thing on each other and on the men at the party.

After putting on their freak show, they started picking out men and asking what they wanted them to do for them and to them. Two strippers took the groom to the bedroom after putting their naked breasts and butts in his face and giving him oral sex right in front of his relatives and friends. There was even a fool there with a video camera who was taping everything.

These black men were crazy and reckless as hell. It was bad enough that they had sex with the strippers, who were total strangers, but recording the performances was total madness. You never know who'll see that tape days, weeks, months, or even years later.

The men had no idea or didn't care that the women had just left a strip club where they were having sex with different men just a few hours earlier. Some of the strippers even charged extra to have sex with them raw. This was insane, no matter how high or drunk you are. These were strippers aka hookers who danced and had sex for money.

I couldn't understand it. These black men seemed oblivious. They could easily have contracted an STD or HIV/AIDs. They acted as if they didn't care. Not only were they running the risk of infection; they were putting their wives and girlfriends at risk.

I ended up doing about a dozen more bachelor parties before I stopped for good. Almost all the parties were the same. The black men and the groom came to these parties for sex and engaged in one kind of sex or another with the strippers.

Most of the strippers and dancers at the bachelor parties where I worked security were black women, although there were a few Latinas. All the parties, however, were held for black men. Many of the strippers used to tell me that they hated doing parties for black men because they demanded all kinds of freaky things for little money. They loved to do parties for white men, and black ballers, hustlers, or drug dealers because the money was nothing to them.

Black women, I told you that I was going to give it to you straight and uncut. A lot of crazy stuff goes on at bachelor parties and in strip clubs, and you need to know about it. Not all my observations come from my experiences working strip clubs or bachelor parties. A good deal I gathered from black men. They talked about their exploits at bachelor parties with pride and excitement. They would brag about what they did with this stripper or that one. Some even took pictures, and one fool showed them to us at work. Often the other men listening would cheer them on because the stories were so wild.

One black man that I worked with brought the video taken at a bachelor party to the jobsite for everyone to watch. Not only did this man have the nerve to show the tape to strangers he had just met on the job, he was showing them a tape of his own bachelor party. Just a few weeks before he had been handing around pictures he had taken on his honeymoon.

How can you go into church and pledge to love someone through sickness and health, forsaking all others when less than twenty-four hours before you'd gone fucking wild and had sex with a stranger for money. Black men are just lying to themselves if they think that having a strange woman's breast, ass, or coochie in their hands and faces will strengthen their will to be faithful once they're married. The big lie they tell themselves is that they're getting fooling around out of their system. Yeah, right.

How can any black man honestly think a marriage has a chance of success when it begins after a night of crazy sex with a stranger? His conscious and subconscious thoughts will be on the wild escapades he had less than twenty-four hours before. That man may love you, but he's not ready to be faithful to one woman. He might mouth the words, but his heart and his loins say something else.

A black man can love a woman and still have sex with another. It's a lust and a desire thing—and he's not willing to give up his player ways. A lot of times it's a momentary pursuit of pleasure and satisfaction.

As I mentioned earlier, my father was playing games and cheating on my mother before they were married and while they were married. He's remarried, but hasn't given up playing his games. Many black men, like my father, never change their player ways.

The bachelor party tradition is a big joke and a big lie. First, the bachelor party is a tradition established by white men in Europe and America. It didn't become part of the black marriage rituals until around the time of affirmative action. Second, the bachelor party, in the black interpretation, is a lie because it has become synonymous with a sex party and makes a mockery of marriage vows.

Half of all marriages end in divorce in the first two years. I can relate to those statistics because that's what happened to my marriage. A lot of black men get married knowing that they are not ready to stop being players. They want to have their cake and eat it too. Until black men give up the games before they get married, we will have more divorces within the first two years of marriage.

What a black man does at his bachelor party is a prime indicator of whether he's committed to making the marriage work and willing to give up his games and playing around. A friend asked me to be in his wedding, and the bachelor party told me the marriage was destined to fail, even if it didn't end in divorce within two years.

I was good with being asked to be a groomsman because I'd known him for years. We were close, at least I thought we were. A week before the wedding, he called me and asked me to pick him up at the house where he lived with his fiancée. When I pulled up, he was already standing outside waiting for me.

After getting into my SUV, he started talking about his doubts— he wasn't not sure about getting married; he'd been having a lot of arguments with his fiancée lately. Then he asked me what I thought about her. I told him that he had it made. She had a good career, a wonderful personality; she was dependable, a great cook, and, on top of that, she was funny. Most of all, I said , she loved him through and through.

"Yeah, you're right," he said, "she is something special and she do love me, and I know I'll never find no one who'll love me like she does, and she'll always have my back no matter what I do."

A few days before the wedding I got a call from him telling me that his cousin, who was his best man, was throwing a bachelor party for him and I had to come. The bachelor party was going to be held at one of the best hotels in the city. I told him that I had to be at work early in the morning and couldn't make it. He was adamant that I come; all the groomsmen were going to be there. I gave in and told him I'd be there, but could only stay for a few hours.

When I got home later, it was another story. My lady had strong objections. She had never liked or trusted my friend; she said he looked sneaky. And she wasn't feeling me going to any bachelor party where there would be naked women shaking their breasts and asses in my face. I had never told my lady about my past jobs doing security for strippers and dancers at bachelor parties and thought it best to keep quiet as the relationship was already on shaky ground.

Believe it or not, I really didn't want to go to the bachelor party. For one thing, my lady disapproved and was mouthing off about it and giving me the cold shoulder. I also didn't feel like being around a bunch of naked men and women. Last but not least, I was tired from working at the construction site and just wanted to get some sleep.

The night of the bachelor party my lady dropped me off at the hotel and told me sarcastically to behave myself. I laughed and said I wouldn't be staying long and would give her a call to pick me up. When I got to the suite, the groom greeted me with a big smile and introduced me to everyone I didn't know. There were a lot of black women in the suite, and I asked my friend if they were the strippers. He shook his head. No, they were his cousin's friends and a few women he knew from work.

This was something new to me—women at a bachelor party who were not strippers or dancers. None of them were members of the wedding party, however, and none of the men had invited their wives or girlfriends. I've subsequently discovered that this is an unwritten etiquette for bachelor parties.

My friend's bachelor party was more like a get-together or a private party than the ones I'd worked. The women were just chilling—talking and laughing it up. Everyone was drinking liquor, smoking blunts, eating, or watching an X-rated movie. I found a spot on one of the twin beds and fell asleep, waiting for the strippers to show up.

The sounds of female voices woke me up. I was thinking it was about time the strippers got there because it was getting late. But it was only more women guests coming in, carrying trays of food and bags filled with liquor bottles.

I told my friend I was leaving. I wasn't going to stay any longer and break my promise to my lady. I didn't need or want any drama in my world. He was disappointed and said I was about to miss all the fun. But before I left, he said, I had to meet someone special. Then he introduced me to a very sexy, beautiful black woman who could have passed for Janet Jackson when she was in her twenties.

My friend had met her a few weeks earlier. I could tell by the way he was acting that he was lusting hard for her. On the way to the door, he couldn't stop talking about her—how she owned a hair salon, drove a brand-new Benz, and was making money hand over fist. For a man who was getting married in less than thirty-six hours to a woman he'd lived with for three years, he sure was excited about this woman he'd known for a few weeks.

Walking out through the lobby, I ran into the strippers who were headed to the party. I could see my lady was already parked out front, watching me like a hawk. Once I got into the SUV she asked if I'd seen enough ass and whether I wanted to go back to the suite.

The next day I got a phone call from my friend, the groom, to tell me that I shouldn't have left the party. The strippers were off the hook. Then he gave me a blow-by-blow description of what happened. After the strippers left about 4:00 a.m. and everyone else had fallen asleep, he'd ended up on one of the twin beds having sex with the woman he'd introduced me to.

This fool stayed out the whole night and never went home to his fiancée until the next morning. I'm shaking my head while he's telling me about all the fun he had with her. I'm thinking that he has everything a black man could want in his life—a beautiful, loving fiancée, with a great career, a big house in a nice neighborhood—yet this fool was more excited about having sex with a woman he met a few week earlier than about his wedding.

It's bad enough that he cheated on his wife-to-be the night before the weeding. It's pitiful to have no shame or guilt about it. He was actually feeling proud of cheating, which, to me, is worse than the act itself.

Any black woman would have legitimate grounds for doubting whether or not she should go through with a wedding to a man whose mind was on a sexy lady he'd had sex with the night before or on strippers who gave oral sex like no woman had ever given him before, or the two strippers who were all over him and he couldn't wait to call when he got back from his honeymoon.

Black men like these don't give their marriages a fighting chance. My friend even had the audacity to invite the woman he'd had sex with to his wedding reception. He asked me to go over and meet her girlfriend, but I was finished with him and just wanted to get away from the masquerade. That day I lost all the respect I had for him. I thought his wife was something special. While the wedding pictures were being taken, it was hard for me to smile, knowing what I knew about her new husband.

After years of running night clubs and doing security for strip clubs and bachelor parties, I can only conclude that bachelor parties are a hazard. They are set up to benefit the men who are married or in serious relationship more than the groom although the groom can get entangled, as my erstwhile friend did. Bachelor parties give them an excuse, and the opportunity, to cheat on their wives and girlfriends with strippers and a reason to stay out all night.

I've talked to more than a thousand black men over the years and asked them how long it took after they got married for them to start having desire for other women or creeping on their wives. In interviews I used the word "creeping" because a lot of black men get sensitive when you use "cheating" or "adultery." However sensitive they are to the terminology, it's still adultery. It's still cheating.

The answers of majority of them who had had bachelor parties ranged from three weeks to four months. But for most of those who had not had bachelor parties the range was four to five years and a lot of them said never. That's why I believe bachelor parties are harmful to a new marriage. The combination of hard liquor, marijuana, and butt-naked strippers is a recipe for disaster, especially when drunken family members and friends egg the groom on. How much resistance can a groom or any other man put up?

A lot of black men have the fantasy of having sex with two women at the same time, and a bachelor party gives them the opportunity to fulfill that fantasy. Who knows how long a man can or will resist? Some bachelor parties are so off the hook that they qualify as orgies—where black men take turns with strippers as long as the money is right.

Now that you know what goes on at a lot of bachelor parties, you will know the deal when your fiancé or husband comes to you and talks about having or going to a bachelor party. When and if you decide to tell him what you have heard and read about what really goes on at a bachelor party, he will most likely tell you that it's all lies. The bachelor party he's going to or having won't be anything like that, just a little lap dancing—like he can really control what other black men want to do when they're surrounded by hot, sexy, naked strippers.

If you ask your fiancé, husband or boyfriend not to go to or have a bachelor party, he will probably get upset and turn the request into an argument. I'm willing to bet that 90 percent will refuse. Then it's time to test his sincerity. If he insists on going to or having a bachelor party, ask if you and your girlfriends and female relatives can come. He will definitely be caught off guard, and you will have a moment of silence. He will need a few seconds or minutes to think of what to say.

One of two things will most likely happen. Either he'll throw his hands up and say that he's not going or having one if he has put up with all this drama or he'll tell you that you can't come because it's for men only.

This is another big lie. Ask around your local hair or beauty salon. The women who work in salons know what's going on better than anyone when it comes to black men. Just because he told you he wasn't going to a bachelor party or not having one doesn't mean he's going to keep his word.

The good, caring, and understanding black man will respect your wishes because he loves you and cares about your feelings—and because he knows that peace and love in marriage are priceless compared to one night of pleasure.

You are still going to have grooms who want something special before the wedding. Have a "Before Wedding Party," for adults only, where you can get your drink on, your dance on, let your hair down and have a ball. You're not going to be able to party like you want and drink like you want, and listen to the music you want to listen to at the reception. Young children and older adults will be there, and you have to take wedding pictures after the ceremony.

So it's not a bad idea to have a "Before Wedding Party" or whatever you want to call it. It's certainly better for your future happiness in marriage than a bachelor party.

A selfish black man will want to do what pleases him with no regard for you and your marriage or relationship—and that includes what goes on at a bachelor party. A good man knows how to listen to what you have to say and is sensitive to what your feelings when it comes to your marriage and relationship.

Chapter 12

The 52 Fake-Out

Always remember that you are unique, one of a kind. That your wonderful, beautiful, loving presence is a present to this world. Always know that your life can be anything you want it to be as long as you set your heart and mind to it. Black women, you're so beautiful, like the stars in the sky. Always be grateful to each day you are blessed to see, no matter how hard life may be for you because with faith and patience come ease and happiness—not always when you want,
but they will come. As long as you stay strong and count your blessings and not your troubles, you'll make it through whatever life brings your way. Within you are so many answers. Don't put limits on yourself, on what you can and cannot do. Have courage and be strong because there are so many dreams waiting to be realized.

The 52 Fake-Out is another hot subject. It's about the engagement ring games that a lot of black men play. I call them the "52 Fake-Out" because black men play them in so many ways to fake you out, to make you believe that they really want to marry you.

I discovered the 52 Fake-Out before I was married. I noticed a lot of black women I was meeting were engaged, but didn't have engagement rings or they had engagements rings but had been engaged for two, three, or four years with no wedding date set. This seemed crazy to me. When I asked my ex-wife to marry me, we were married five months later.

Let's be honest. Do you really believe that a man who claims to love a woman is going to wait three or four years to marry her? He already has the best of both worlds. He has a woman who's engaged to him; he doesn't have to worry about her going anywhere or seeing another man, and he doesn't have to spend a dime on a wedding ceremony. He has all the benefits of being married without the legal tie or strings. He has it made. He has the cake and ice cream, and he can eat all he wants when he wants.

Almost all the women who had engagement rings had known their fiancés for a few years, and many had a child or children by them. Some of these women got their rings only when they were on the verge of leaving their boyfriends or child's fathers, when they saw no future in the relationship and wanted to date other men. Other black women would get engagement rings, but then wait years without a wedding date on the horizon.

Any woman who is supposedly engaged, but has no engagement ring or fixed date for the wedding has to question whether she's really engaged and her so-called fiancé really intends to marry her.

Most of the black women that I have talked to about being engaged but who were still waiting for engagement rings were between the ages of eighteen and thirty, and the younger they were, the most likely it was that they would fall for the engagement ring games. Older black women aren't so often taken in by a lot of the games black men play because they've been there before.

The engagement ring games are played every day everywhere, yet most women don't have a clue about them. A black woman I met by chance in Wal-Mart's is a good illustration of how easy it is to be caught in the 52-Fake-Out if you don't know it's being played on you. After I introduced myself to her, she rushed to tell me, before I could chat her up, that she was engaged. I apologized and said that I wouldn't have tried to talk to her had I known she was engaged. I didn't see a ring and just assumed she wasn't.

I asked her if she'd mind telling me why she was engaged with no ring. She told me with a little attitude that her fiancé hadn't picked out her ring yet. I then asked her how long she had been engaged. She told me for almost a year. I tried not to laugh, but I couldn't help smiling. I'd heard similar stories from various women over the past few years.

When she saw me smiling, she got defensive and said she had wondered about it, had even asked him a few times when he was going to give her a ring. One time he told her that he had to get his car serviced and inspected. Another time, he said he was saving up to buy her a really special ring.

After telling her I was writing a book about relationships, she opened up although she still had a little attitude and was adamant that her fiancé loved her and wasn't playing games with her. He wanted to marry her just as much as she wanted to marry him. I asked if her fiancé had a good job and his own apartment, whether he dressed in the latest gear and went out to night clubs and strip clubs. She got impatient with the questions; the answer to all of them was obviously yes.

Let me get to the point, I said. If your fiancé has a nice paying job and works a forty-hour week, he probably makes about five or six hundred dollars a week after taxes. That comes to twenty-six thousand a year, give or take a thousand. Say his rent is eight hundred a month. That's twenty-six hundred; throw in three thousand for utilities and five for personal expenses. With his income and expenses, he still has plenty left over. He can easily pick out a nice one-carat princess-cut diamond engagement ring that costs as little as thirty-five hundred.

She looked stunned as the realization hit. If he really wanted to marry her the way he said he did, he would have bought her a ring by now. He could have used all the money he spent on new gear or at night clubs.

There's no excuse for a man not to buy you an engagement ring or at least put money down on one within six months to a year of proposing. Otherwise he should wait to propose. That's what most men do when they really want to get married. This is where the lies and the games start in a relationship, if they haven't already started. For an engagement to be official, there has to be an engagement ring. Don't let any man play you and make you think otherwise.

How can you discover whether your fiancé is really sincere about marrying you or just playing games when you find yourself in a situation similar to the Wal-Mart lady's.

The next time you see your fiancé, come right out and ask when you're going to get your ring. If he tells you soon, you should press him. How soon? If he says in a few months, don't be placated. If you really want to test his intentions, tell him that men have been coming on to you lately, trying to get your name and number and don't believe you when you say you're engaged because you're not wearing a ring.

Tell him you feel like a fool. It's been almost a year. If he doesn't get you a ring by the end of the month, you are no longer going to consider yourself engaged and are going to start dating other men. Most likely he will get defensive and plead for more time. But if he loves you and really wants to marry you, a month shouldn't be a problem. The ball is in his court.

You should keep the conversation short and sweet. The longer you talk to him about it, the more excuses he'll come up with to explain why he can't get you a ring and why you should wait longer. Drop the topic and just go about your everyday business, maybe even plan more nights out with your girlfriends so you are not so available to him.

My Wal-Mart lady did exactly what I've described. A few weeks later, I received a phone call from her. Her fiancé had given her a two-carat diamond ring. I warned her not to let the engagement drag on for another couple of years without a wedding date being set. She told me that she wasn't going to let that happen. She realized after her fiancé gave her the engagement ring that she had just as much say in what direction their relationship took as he did.

Not all engagement games turn out so well. Every situation with a black man is different, particularly when children and ex-girlfriends are involved. Another woman I counseled had been engaged for over two years and still didn't have an engagement ring. Her fiancé had a good job, his own apartment, and had bought a new car the year before. He also had a child by his ex-girlfriend.

The couple spent almost all their time at her apartment. When she suggested staying over at his apartment, he would tell her that she couldn't because his son was there. He explained that he was trying to keep the peace with the boy's mother so she wouldn't take him to court for child support and get full custody.

The woman took my advice and, like the Wal-Mart lady, issued an ultimatum: a ring or the engagement was off. When she confronted her fiancé about her engagement ring, things didn't work out as she had hoped and they broke up. But she was happy, she said. She was busy getting her life back on track.

She had been lying to herself for a long time and felt something wasn't right in their relationship. She had driven over to his place to talk to him about the engagement ring. She hadn't called to let him know that she was coming over the way she usually did. When she got to his apartment, she went straight to his door and rang the bell. While she was waiting for him to answer, all kinds of thoughts were running through her mind. He had the keys to her place and could come by whenever he felt like it, but she didn't have keys to his place and had to call ahead whenever she wanted to come by. When he opened the door, the first thing out of his mouth was why didn't she call before she came over. He was about to leave to take his son to a doctor's appointment with the boy's mother.

The whole time he was talking to her, her stomach kept flipping like crazy. She wasn't going to let him get away that easily so she asked him to step outside. Couldn't wait until later, he asked. She said no. Something, she knew, was very wrong. It was as if he was trying to hide her and didn't want anyone to hear what they were talking about.

They got into her car and she told him how she felt about not having an engagement ring for the two years they'd been engaged, how he had keys to her place and could drop by anytime he liked, but she had to call before coming over to his apartment. He told her that he had a lot of bills to pay and was giving his son's mother money to help take care of his son. He wasn't going to let anyone or anything come between him and his son, and he couldn't think about marriage until he got things straightened out with his son's mother about custody and child support. He took the keys to her apartment off his keychain and gave them back to her, telling her that he'd call her later.

Two month later she still hadn't heard from him. But she's no longer stuck in a relationship that was going nowhere. Many black men have women sitting around while they go on with their lives, doing whatever they like with whomever they like. They might have sincere intentions in the beginning of a relationship, but over time things change. Pressure builds: A child's mother can threaten to take them to court for more support or for full custody. Maybe they are still having sex with an ex-girlfriend. Maybe they simply change their minds about getting married. Or maybe they know exactly what they are doing and just don't care.

In any engagement when your fiancé has a child by another woman it's important to meet the mother. She must know you exist. If you are in a relationship and have never met the mother of your partner's child or you are introduced as a friend, there's something very wrong.. He's just messing around. You should never be thought of or presented as a friend or hidden.

Every situation is different. The Wal-Mart lady's fiancé really loved her, but was dragging his feet. He needed a jump start on his responsibilities in the relationship and a reality check about the consequences of not living up to them and honoring his proposal with a ring. A lot of black men are not as serious about their relationships as he was. They may not be ready for an honest relationship. Or they may have other women or children in their lives and don't want to choose between them and a fiancée. The demand for a ring exposes the men who are playing this game.

Then there are the black women who have engagement rings, but have been waiting for as long as seven years to get married. What's wrong with this picture? A black man will sometimes propose to take his woman out of circulation. She may be feeling that the relationship isn't going anywhere and want more, especially if she's sexually active with him. He doesn't want her dating other men or to lose her. So he proposes, knowing this is what she wants; the engagement keeps her in check and his alone.

Once engaged he doesn't have to worry about anyone else talking to her because she believes her fiancé is sincere about building a future together. This is a heartless game black men play on innocent, loving loyal, and trusting black women. Their thoughts are totally different than those women have when they get engaged.

Many black men get engaged not because they want to get married, but to control their women. Such a man thinks that if she's engaged, she's happy and won't give any other man the time of day. To a lot of black men an engagement acts as a shield, keeping interested men at bay and away. Other black men, like the man with the son, propose with no intention of ever getting married, but to keep their women in their lives as long as possible.

A black woman can waste years of her life on a black man who is playing the 52-Fakeout games, who is neither willing nor ready to commit to a relationship. You're probably wondering why a black man even bothers proposing to a woman if he intends to go on playing the field and fooling around.

First of all he thinks it costs less to be engaged than it does to keep dating. After six months to a year of dating and spending money every time they go out, it adds up. If he's not ready to let her go and end the relationship, he'll propose to keep her in his life, especially is she's a good catch and has her own vehicle, house, money, a good job, and is great in bed. It's a plus if she doesn't have any children and treats him like a king.

Summer is the worst season, the hardest on their pockets, and the most expensive time to date—with vacations, outdoor concerts, and sporting events. Players will get engaged before the weather warms up to slow things down. Once she's engaged, a woman is more likely to be content to stay at his place or with him staying at her apartment just watching television or a movie and cooking for him or ordering out. Some players admitted that they had managed to get away with this game for years. Now and then they would take their women out to dinner, a play, or concert just to make them happy and stop their complaints about never going anywhere

For some players it's about money and control. They don't have to worry about another man hitting on their women and the women become more devoted to them when they think marriage really is in the cards. Players also think that they can get away with more when they're engaged. One player told me that if you spend anywhere from two to five thousand on a ring, you can get away with anything. A two-carat diamond will set him back three to five thousand, little more than he would spend in a few months going to night clubs or sporting events. It's well worth it. He's getting more sex, and she's doing things to him that she never would have done before they were engaged. He didn't care that she opened up with him, became freer, because she actually believed they would be married.

As a black woman, you must beware of players who propose just so you won't leave them or to save money and then leave you in limbo for months or years without a ring or a wedding date. If he doesn't have an engagement ring when he proposes, you shouldn't accept. Tell him that you will give him your answer once he has a ring for you. His reaction will reveal his true intentions. If he asks you why you can't give him an answer right then, tell him a ring makes the proposal special and official. If he fades into the woodwork, he was most likely playing a 52-Fake-Out on you. The next time you see him, he will act as if he never proposed to you. You should follow suit and pretend it never happened.

Once you are engaged, keep on your fiancé about setting a wedding date. If he's sincere about marrying you, and loves you like he says, you shouldn't have to wait years for the wedding. Realistically a wedding date should be set within six months to a year after your engagement. If it's longer than that, you might be setting yourself up for a big letdown.

A ring and a wedding date shouldn't cause problems for a man who really wants to get married, who loves you, and wants you for his wife.

Chapter 13

Sports Night Out

We black men are funny creatures when it comes to what we want and need in our lives. Sometimes we don't even know until it's too late. Bear with us because most of us are good men. We just have issues that we have to deal with from time to time.

Most black men love sports; some even put sporting events ahead of their wives and girlfriends. They will pick an argument or turn a deaf ear to objections in order to go out to sports bars or take in a game or fight with hommies and relatives.

I used to follow sports with a passion, but then my addiction got me sleeping alone or on the sofa. I was late coming home or sometimes out all night. Sports were all I knew growing up. They were in my blood and provided an outlet for a lot of the anger and frustration I was dealing with.

I played almost everything. But I didn't just play; I also watched every sporting event I could with the same passion that I played. And I gambled on them. Playing, watching, and gambling went hand in hand. Playoff times in the NBA, NFL, NHL, or NCAA, when my team was going for the championship, were the most intense.

To make sure I knew all I could about the teams and the players before placing my bet, I would buy every sports magazine or paper I could. I watched ESPN and other sport show religiously. I devoured any information that would help me pick my winners.

I was so good at picking winning teams that my friends and co-workers would call me for advice about game and fights. If they won, they would usually give me some money for the tip.

Being heavily into the sports scene, it was impossible not to notice that married or attached black men used sports bars not only to catch an event, but to pick up women. Many told me that their wives or girlfriends didn't like watching sports with them, so meeting other women at sports bars was easy.

Initially a man might go to a sports bar to watch a game or fight, to get his drink on, and to hang out with family members and friends, but while he's chilling and watching the game or fight, he'd meet women who were into sports as much as he was. The man would start chatting up one of them and discover they had a lot in common. One thing would lead to another, and casual chance meetings turned into regular occurrences. Pretty soon he was seeing the woman after the games or going over to her apartment. You know the rest.

Sometimes the man even stopped going to the sports bar. Instead, after lying to his wife or girlfriend about going out to watch a game or a fight, he'd meet the new woman and they did their thing.

The players in the sports bar scene never worry that their wives or girlfriend will come in and discover they are fooling around or not there. As a rule, their wives or girlfriends are not into sports and would rather be doing something else. When they do take their wives or girlfriends, the women can't wait to get out of there. They grab the keys to the car or truck and leave early.

Nor do the players worry that their wives' relatives or friends will see them with another woman. Sports bars are always crowded, and it' impossible to tell which customers have hooked up unless they come in or leave together. Everyone leaves at the end of a game, anyways, unless it's a blowout and there's not enough time left for your team to win. Any player is smart enough not to make physical contact with the other woman; he won't chance being caught fooling around by someone snapping pictures with a cell phone camera.

Many of the black men I've talked to complained that their wives or girlfriends made no effort to learn about the various sports. The majority would have loved to share sporting events with them. Hanging out with family or friends was okay, but nothing compared to watching a game or fight with wives or girlfriends who loved sports as much as they did. Many of the black men told me that they never planned on meeting other women at sports bars, but before they knew it, they were caught up in an affair or having a one-night stand.

Black women do come to sports bars, either alone or with girlfriends. Even though most of the crowd in a sports bar is dressed casually—team sweatshirts or jerseys, jeans, and sneakers—certain women wear sexy clothes. They dress that way, they told me, to attract the attention of the men. A half-dressed female can usually distract a man, even when he's heavily into watching a game or fight. These playettes are out sports-bar hopping, hoping to catch a baller or player. They operate in a similar fashion to the groupies that frequent rap concerts. They know all the best sports bars to meet men, especially ballers and players. They even alert one another on their cell phones when a baller or player comes into a sports bar.

These female players or sports groupies fall into one of three categories.

Category #1. This is the most active contingent. It's made up of women between the ages of eighteen and thirty-six. They are single, single mothers, employed or unemployed, with their own apartment or house or living with a relative or girlfriend.

Category #2. Female players in this group are between twenty- one and forty. They are in relationships, engaged, or married. Some of the married women have children, and most are employed.

Category #3. Members of this group are in the minority among sports groupies and are the oldest. Their ages range between thirty-five and forty-nine. They are married, divorced, single, employed or running their own businesses out of their apartments or houses.

They either have no children or their children are in their teen or grown up.

Females in the first category play the game mainly for the money—what the guys they pick up can buy or do for them. They are also into the thrill of catching a baller or player or having someone else's husband or boyfriend chasing after them. Good sex is a bonus for them. Bragging rights are important to these women. Black men aren't the only ones who boast about their conquests and the people they have slept with or are sleeping with.

Women in the second category play the game for the rush of being with men who are different from their husbands or boyfriends and give them the attention that they don't get in their marriages or relationships. They also like the men to take them places and buy things for them or give them money for bills and personal indulgences. But they won't ask for money; they don't want to be thought of as gold diggers, whores, or groupies.

The old playettes make up the third and last category. They have been playing for years and teach the rules to younger female players who are new to the game. Many of them are financially secure. They play the game for the fun of it. They also like the young ballers and players. In fact, they don't differ much from male players who are old hands at the game.

The average black man doesn't know how hard these women plot when they go out to sports bars, A lot of men, perhaps even your husbands or boyfriends, don't stand a chance when these female players come at them strong and hard at a sports bar. They can break a man's will and resistance down like cardboard, especially if he's high or intoxicated and has a half-naked woman in his face. Many men can't help but fall victim to the game; these women play it so well.

But there also plenty of black men who are so into the sports event or fight and so hyped on their team or fighter winning, a sexy half-naked women doesn't faze them. She's more of an annoying distraction when the game or fight is on because they've bet hard and heavy on the outcome.

If you ask your husband or boyfriend if you can go with him to a sports bar, his reaction often throws up warning signs that he may be fooling around there as well as watching a sporting event.

Warning Signs That Something Might Be Going On

1. He gives off a lot of negative vibes when you mention going with him. This might be a sign that he's meeting someone else and never expected you to ask to go with him.
2. He tells you that you won't like the crowd and all the noise.
3. He tells you that he'll take you next time.
4. He starts an argument just so he won't have to take you with him.

All of these warning signs are indications that your husband or boyfriend might be up to something other than watching a game or a fight at a sports bar. A lot of black men are weak as hell when it comes to sexy half-naked women hanging around them. Often they don't plan on meeting another woman; it just happens because they are too weak to resist the temptation. That's no excuse, but it's a fact.

When you get a chance, make time to learn about your husband's or boyfriend's favorite sports team. Watch ESPN and read the sports section of the newspaper occasionally. You can ask a male or female relative or girlfriend who's into sports questions about his favorite teams or fighters. You don't have to get a lot of information. The basics will go a long way in showing your husband or boyfriend that you love him enough to make room in your life for the sports he loves.

You might be thinking: Why should you care or try drum up interest in sports when you don't like them. There's a simple reason. If you love your husband or boyfriend and want your marriage or relationship to survive potential obstacles, then you should take the time to learn about something he is passionate about. Isn't your marriage or relationship worth working on and fighting for?

As a black man, I know we sometimes make the wrong choices and think with our little brains instead of our big brains. This may get us into trouble, but it doesn't always mean that we don't love you. So why give your husband or boyfriend the opportunity to slip up or drop his guard when he's intoxicated. A moment of weakness can lead to other things.

Behind every good black man is a strong, loving black woman. You have to be strong for your husband and boyfriends at times. You cannot just sit back and let whatever happens happen when your marriage or relationship is on the line. You don't have to watch everything your husband or boyfriend does or go everywhere he goes. Just let him know that you're interested in doing things that he loves, then give him space now and then.

You can be a part of your husband or boyfriend's life without crowding him. You can go with him occasionally, not every time, to a sports bar. Showing your face has the added advantage of letting the female players and groupies know that you're on point when it comes to your husband or boyfriend. When you are not around, there will be less chance that they will make a move on him.

It's also important to make your presence known to his friends and co-workers and their wives. When they know who you are, when you're not around, they'll ask about you. Where is she? Why didn't she come to watch the games? When they bring you up in conversations, it gives your husband or boyfriend a reality check and keeps his thoughts on you. It prevents a situation from turning into "out of sight, out of mind."

Chapter 14

The Ex-Wife/Ex-Girlfriend Games

We must remember that love is built over time through mutual care and understanding. It does not happen in a few interactions. Lust, on the other hand, can flare up like a fire and end in an instant. Love is lasting, while lust is temporary. Love is patient, while lust is impatient and impulsive. Love makes you feel whole, joyful, and inspired, while lust offers you only heartache and regret.

An ex-wife or ex-girlfriend can pose a real threat to a marriage or relationship, particularly if she has a child or children from that earlier involvement. Often a black woman puts up with her husband's or boyfriend's continuing contact because she doesn't want to appear jealous or insecure. Such forbearance can prove dangerous.

Rarely does ongoing involvement stop at the bedroom door. Few black men can be friends with their ex-wives, ex-girlfriends, or the mothers of their children. Although any man must meet his obligations to provide spousal or child support and be involved in raising his child, limits should be clearly set so that the arrangements remain on a business level between the man and his ex.

Many black men have told me over the years that they remained friends with former lovers. In far too many cases, "friends" was a euphemism. They were having sex with those "friends," and their wives or girlfriends didn't have a clue. These men would actually trade stories about getting away with having sex with former wives or girlfriends or the mothers of their children. Most wives and girlfriends didn't object, thinking their husbands or boyfriends were simply keeping in touch. If a wife or girlfriend did complain, the man would come up with a good reason why he needed to talk to his ex or she had to call him.

One married man, for example, said his wife didn't mind that he kept in touch with two, yes two, of his ex-girlfriends. In fact, they used to live with him in the house where he, his wife, and children now live. Sometimes when one of his exes called, his wife would answer the phone and chat for a few minutes, as if they were the best of friends, asking how the ex and her children were doing. She had no idea that these exes were snakes out to get what she had.

The man had a handy justification for those calls. He was good at fixing car and trucks. His wife knew this so he worked out an understanding with his ex-girlfriends. When one of them called his house and needed to see him, she was to explain that she was having problems with her car. He'd then tell his wife he had to go over and take a look.

He had the ruse down pat. His ex needed the car to get to work and didn't have the money to take it to a regular repair shop. He would get his tools from the basement, put them in his truck, drive over to her place and have sex.

Because his wife knew he charged everyone to fix a car or truck, no matter who they were, to cover his tracks, he sometimes needed to stop at an ATM machine to take out money to give his wife. Before he went back home, he would put on dirty overalls. Then he'd come into the house with his tools and work clothes on. He'd hand his wife the money, but tell her that his ex still owed him, which gave him an excuse to stop by her place again. He'd take a shower as if he had done nothing but work on a car. He was working all right, but not on his ex's car.

He actually bragged that he'd taken up with his exes only a few months after he got back from his honeymoon. This element of boasting, in fact, characterized most of the conversations I had with black men about their relations with former wives or girlfriends. Not only had they cheated on their wives or girlfriends; they were proud of it and felt no guilt or shame. How ignorant is that—to stoke your ego by advertising to your friends your sexual cheating business? You can fool and lie to others, but you can't fool and lie to yourself.

Not all exes were wives or long-time girlfriends. Sometimes the men rekindled brief affairs. A friend had been married a few weeks, and he was driving his cousin and me around in his brand-new Ford Excursion. The whole time he talked about a woman he'd had sex with at his bachelor party and how he couldn't wait to see her again. He wasn't talking about how wonderful his honeymoon had been or how happy he was to be married. When he did mention his honeymoon, he described the different women on the beach, the fantastic bodies and asses, and how he wished he'd been there by himself.

I shook my head and wondered how I could ever trust this fool in business dealings or anything else when he didn't have any respect or loyalty for a wife that he'd been with for years. If he could lie and cheat on his wife before and after they were married, he could lie and cheat me in our business dealings without blinking an eye. Even while we were riding around, he would pull up every time he saw a nice-looking woman.

Another married black man described to a group of avid listeners the strategy that he used to get away with cheating on his wife with his baby's mother. He had made an agreement with his baby's mother when they separated to give her $500 to $750 a month until his child was eighteen because he didn't want the court system to be in their business. He had explained this agreement to his wife when they first met and she had no problem with it. After he got engaged to his wife, he started having sex with his baby's mother to soften her up so he wouldn't have to pay her all the money he had agreed to give her each month. He needed, after all, to save up for the wedding and honeymoon.

After his wife had their daughter, she didn't want to have sex with him anymore. He would have to beg just for some oral sex. Cut off at home, he went back to his baby's mother and renewed their sexual relations. He would buy clothes, toys, and food just to have a reason to see her for sex. One time he told his wife that his son was sick and he had to pick up a prescription at CVS. As it was late when he left to get the medicine, he ended up spending the night. When he came home in the morning, his wife merely asked how his son was feeling.

No matter how much you trust your husband or boyfriend, it's not just him that you have to worry about. Black women have a lot of game when they want to have sex with a man. A former wife or girlfriend often remembers how good the sex was and wants it again. She will at least test the waters to see if she can entice him back into her bed.

I've talked to black women who have described how they played men to get what they wanted when they wanted it. Many ex-wives and ex-girlfriends can be merciless and relentless. Because it's impossible to know an ex's motivation or intentions, you shouldn't let a husband or boyfriend keep in contact with a former lover, not even to wish her a happy birthday. You most definitely don't want to let his ex-lover call your home.

No matter how innocent things might seem to you, the reality may not be so innocent and can lead to not-so-innocent things behind your back. Many ex-lovers will act as spoilers, out of spite. They aren't happy because you're happy and in love with the man that used to be in their lives. They may wonder why they aren't the ones who are happy. Envying your happiness, they may jump at the opportunity to test your marriage or relationship.

Advice on How to Deal with an Ex Who Has Children by Him

1. Have your husband or boyfriend mail the check or money order for child support to her or the courts. Anything extra can be sent by mail.
2. When your husband or boyfriend has to pick up his child or children for visitation, try to go with him as often as possible so your presence can be known and felt.
3. Any phone call from the mother of your husband's or boyfriend's baby should concern his child or children. Try not to let her pull him into personal business that has nothing to do with his responsibilities as a father.

Almost every black woman that I talked to had a husband or boyfriend who kept in touch with his former lover. They hated it. It made them mad as hell when they walked into a room and discovered their husband or boyfriend on the phone talking to his ex-wife or ex-girlfriend. Sometimes they couldn't help but be curious and would eavesdrop. They could tell he wasn't talking about anything important—just her personal business. That inevitably sparked an argument.

The wives and girlfriends would object to an ex calling whenever she wanted just to see how he was doing. They thought it was disrespectful. Some of them told me that he would get defensive— say that he'd known his ex's family a long time or that they were talking about a friend or family member who was sick or had passed away. There was no reason for her to be jealous or feel insecure; that he loved only her, and he wasn't fooling around with his ex.

The majority of women dealing with this situation said it didn't seem right that their husbands or boyfriends dismissed their concern as if it was no big thing how they felt. Any wife or girlfriend distressed about the role an ex-lover is playing in her husband's or boyfriend's life should make it clear that it *is* a big deal.

When former lovers are part of the equation, you should test your husband or boyfriend by explaining how you feel about any ongoing contact. It's a bad sign if he immediately gets defensive without even hearing you out or thinking about what you are asking him. He might not be the man you think he is. No man is perfect, but you want a man in your life that you can trust. Without trust you have nothing special, no matter how great the sex is or how much money he spends on you. An understanding, loving black man will understand your worries and do what's best for his marriage or relationship.

Chapter 15

Guess Who's Coming to Dinner

Don't let any man rob you of your happiness and joy.
Don't let any man leave you bitter when he' off somewhere enjoying his life. You need a man who completes you
and makes you strong when you're feeling weak.
Life is too hard to handle alone. You want someone who loves you,
not just lusts for you. Once lust is gone, he's gone.
Forgiveness removes fear; forgiveness gives you back control over your life; forgiveness gives you power over your life.
Hate and fear give him power over
your feelings, thoughts, and actions
—so don't give him that control and free yourself of him.

That half-sister, aunt, or cousin who's come to live with you may not be your husband's or boyfriend's relation after all. This is a big game that's being played on a lot of kindhearted and trusting black women. Out of the blue, a so-called relative you've never heard about shows up and needs to move in with you until she gets back on her feet.

This game is only played on a woman who is not close to her husband's or boyfriend's family and doesn't know many of his relatives. That makes it easy to say his half-sister, aunt, or cousin is coming to town. Is it okay for her to stay with us? he asks. He knows that his wife, being the kind and generous woman she is, will agree without a second thought. The big lie is that so-called relative is the other woman he's been seeing on the side. By masquerading the other woman as a half-sister, aunt, or cousin, he can have his cake and eat it anytime he wants.

Because the wife or girlfriend is not close to his family or doesn't know all his relatives, she cannot call to check on this mystery relative. She takes his word that the woman is who he says she is and welcomes her with open arms. But for a player to pull off the game, the other woman has to be down with the whole charade.

One black man, for example, was having problems with his wife. After she had a miscarriage, she didn't want to have sex with him. On the rare occasions when she was willing, she just lay there on the bed, stiff as a board. He said it was as if all the passion had vanished.

One night while hanging out at a night club, he met a pretty black woman who was about ten years younger than his wife. Tired of his wife's rejection, he ended up having an affair with the woman from the club. She was so nice, he said, he felt as if he had known her for years. She understood what he was going through with his wife and she was there for him.

After seeing her for a few months on the side, she started having money problems. At first he helped her out with her bills, but then his own bills began to pile up. That's when he came up with the idea of telling his wife that his female cousin was getting evicted from her apartment in a few weeks, and he wanted to let her stay with them until she got her own place.

He told his wife that his cousin could give her a break around the house, helping out with the cooking and cleaning. What cousin was he talking about? his wife asked. My first cousin by my father's sister's daughter, he replied with a straight face. When his wife wondered why he hadn't mentioned her before, he told her that they'd lost touch for a long time. His wife finally agreed, but only on the condition that she meet his cousin beforehand.

When the other woman met his wife, they hit it off better than he expected; his wife even helped her move her personal things into their place and the big items and furniture into storage. The other woman ended up living with them for almost a year. He would have sex with her when his wife was at work or out of the house.

Everyone was getting along fine, but then his brother came to visit from out of town. When his brother found out about his "cousin," he was flabbergasted at the arrangement. "You're crazy to take a chance like that. What if mom comes to visit?" he demanded. "Not much chance of that," the man replied. "She doesn't visit anymore. I go over to her house. She blames my wife for losing the baby, thinks she worked too much while she was pregnant."

The craziness is not the risk he ran of getting caught. What is really insane is how brazenly he exploited his wife's generous nature. Black men like him take being a player to a whole new level these days. A lot of men play for keeps, while others play to get all they can out of a woman. They suck her dry—mentally, physically, and financially—then they're on to the next woman. Often they exercise as little judgment as restraint in selecting their next victim.

A co-worker of mine at the record label I was managing in Philadelphia even had the balls to bring home a woman he had met that day after she had spent the night in jail.

He was in his SUV when he caught sight of this sexy black female at a pay phone. There was something about her—he just had to stop and get her name and phone number. When he pulled up, he noticed that she looked stressed and sad. He asked her if she was okay, and she told him that she needed a ride to her girlfriend's place.

He was headed in that direction so he gave her a lift. Once she was in his SUV, he realized she was even sexier that he first thought. They started talking on the ride to her girlfriend's place. He found out that she had just left the police station, where she had been locked up overnight for shoplifting at the Franklin Mills Mall. He was a lifesaver for picking her up, she said. All her money was in her coat, which she had left in her girlfriend's car. A few days before, she and her girlfriend had been at the mall stealing clothes, but the coat she stole was the wrong size. When they went back to exchange it for the right size, a cashier from one of the other stores she had stolen from recognized her and called mall security. The police came and handcuffed her. She was held in the jail overnight, charged with shoplifting, and released on her own recognizance after a court date was set.

To make matters worse, while she was in jail, her cousin had moved out of the apartment that they shared without paying the rent. They paid month by month and were already behind. The landlord threatened to put her things out on the streets if she didn't remove them that night.

My friend felt sorry for her and offered to help her out. He had no money to get her a motel room so he asked her to stay with him and his girlfriend. Even though they had just met, he could tell she was feeling him like he was feeling her. She surprised him by telling him that she was feeling him more than he knew, but she didn't want him to think she was trying to play him because she was in a tough spot.

He told her that he would tell his girlfriend everything that had happened to her, but that she was his cousin. Since his girlfriend knew no one in his family, she wouldn't be suspicious. He called his girlfriend—he'd been living with her for almost two years—and got the green light from her.

Once he introduced his so-called cousin to his girlfriend, they hit it right off. After his girlfriend went to sleep that night, he had sex with the new girl in the living room on the pull-out sofa bed. He didn't worry about his girlfriend waking up and catching them. A train could run through the house, and she wouldn't wake up.

The new girl moved out after staying with them for a month. To this day, his girlfriend still asks about his so-called cousin. He doesn't see the woman anymore. It was just a lust thing between them. He realized that after having sex with her.

There are a few signs to look for that might help you notice when a man, like my co-worker, is trying to play you and pass off his side dish as a relative.

Warning Signs That She's Not Who He Says She Is

1. Beware of the half-sister, aunt, or cousin you've never heard of who suddenly pops up and needs a place to stay.
2. When you ask for information about this relative, your husband or boyfriend gets defensive.
3. When you feel something isn't right, and you call or talk to members of your husband's or boyfriend's family or circle of friends, no one has ever heard of this so-called relative.
4. When holiday events come around, the "relative" can't go. (She has other plans, etc., etc.)
5. Your husband or boyfriend stops having any of his relatives or friends over to the house.

This situation may not apply to you; but it might apply to someone that you know and love. If you have a relative or friend whose husband or boyfriend is taking advantage of her and passing off his other woman as a relation, give her this book to read. Without saying a word or causing any awkwardness between you, you can help alert her. She can then find out for herself the truth about the so-called relative and do what's best for her peace of mind.

Chapter 16

The Live-In Female Relative

Back in the days of a lot of our parents, and our parents' parents, and their parents' parents, black women met black men and fell in love, and black men met black women and fell in love. They got married and had a family together. But nowadays everything has changed, often for the worse. Now you have online dating, and everyone is sleeping around. They've given up courting and marrying. Why buy the cow when you can get all the milk you want for free? Why would your boyfriend or the man that you're seeing want to marry you when he's getting everything from you that a married man gets from his wife? Make a man wait and earn your love and respect. Remember, a black man, young or old, loves a challenge. Don't make it easy for him.

That snake in your garden may not be a convenient half-sister or cousin your husband or boyfriend makes up. It may be one of your own relatives. Inviting a female relation to stay with you can bring trouble into your household from a quarter you never expected—your own family. One woman I talked to let her mother move in after her house caught fire only to discover later that her mother had repaid her kindness by having sex with her boyfriend. She and the boyfriend are no longer together, and she swears she will never trust her mother or any other woman around her man again.

It would never have occurred to many of the husbands and boyfriends involved in these situations to fool around with a partner's relative had she not been right there, living with them. One black man's wife insisted on having her sister move in with them because she was getting a divorce from her abusive husband. The sister-in-law had a five-year-old son who could play with their four-year-old son.

For the first five months, the arrangement worked seamlessly. The sister-in-law was a great cook, much better than his wife, and the kids got along great. Then his wife started taking night classes three times a week. When he got home from the office, the sister-in- law would have dinner ready, the house nice and clean, and the boys bathed and in bed. The two of them would eat dinner together and talk about their day. She even made a terrific desert every night.

Most of the time when his wife came home, she was tired and, after showering, went right to bed. He knew better than to wake her for some loving. They'd already had that argument, and he didn't relish being accused of selfishness. He could hear it now: "All you think about is your needs and wants. You know I've been working and studying all day and all night." The days his wife didn't have class, she would be busy studying.

Nightly sex was a thing of the past when his wife started going to college. One night his sister-in-law told him that he looked sexually frustrated. Her statement caught him off guard. He didn't think it was that obvious.

She just smiled and told him that she felt sorry for his predicament. She confessed that she was also frustrated and tired of playing with herself. When she asked him if he played with himself, he was insulted. He hadn't masturbated since he was a teenager; that's what girlfriends and wives were for. She laughed and left the room. He went back to watching the movie, but she came back a few minutes later, wearing a revealing nightgown, and sat down beside him on the sofa. He'd never paid much attention to her body until then. She usually wore sweatpants, sweatshirts, long-sleeve t-shirts, and baggy jeans.

The sister-in-law got up and went into the kitchen and returned with two glasses of wine—something else she had never done before. They went back to watching the movie, but he found himself getting really comfortable with her lying near him on the sofa. The next thing he knew, they were having sex right there on the sofa. He couldn't help himself—she was that sexy and knew how to make him feel so good. He ended up having sex with her for over a year before she moved out. He was relieved when she finally got a place of her own because she made him feel weak and reminded him of his wife physically.

Often a female relative moves on a husband or boyfriend when she moves in simply by making his life easier—taking care of the kids, cleaning the house, cooking, and sharing expenses. Another black man got a call from his fiancée. Her aunt, who was in a halfway house, needed a place to stay before they would release her. The aunt had a job and could help out with the bills. Besides, they had a spare room. When he asked why her aunt had been locked up, his fiancée told him that she had done four years for bank fraud. Not wanting to hurt his fiancée's feelings, he said okay.

He assumed that the aunt would be an older lady, about the same age as his fiancée's mother. When he got home from work, he found the aunt unpacking in the spare room and was surprised at how young and sexy she was. She couldn't have had more than ten years on him. She gave him a big hug and kiss. The halfway house was driving her crazy, she said. She needed to get out of there before she exploded. She told him that she had money saved and would help out with the bills as well as the cooking and cleaning up around the house.

His fiancée worked from ten in the morning until six in the evening. Usually she didn't get home until after seven. He worked construction from 6:30 a.m. until 2:30 p.m. and then picked up their two-year-old daughter from daycare. Now that the aunt was staying with them, they could save the money they spent on daycare. The aunt could watch their daughter during the day because she worked the night shift.

The arrangement worked out great. They were saving money and when he got home from work, the house would be clean and dinner waiting in the kitchen.

The aunt was very outgoing. When he was sore after a day on the construction site, she would make him take a hot bath and put some nice smelling salts in that relaxed his muscles. It was nice, he said, having someone cater to him after a hard day at work in the hot sun. His fiancée was sweet, but she never catered to him the say her aunt did. She was always busy with office work or taking care of their daughter. Until her aunt moved in, he was lucky to get a shower before his fiancée came home from work.

Gradually the aunt stepped up her campaign. When his fiancée wasn't around, she would walk around the house half-naked, wearing a wife beater and low-cut shorts that left little to the imagination. After being locked up for four years and out for almost eight months, she'd had sex only twice, she told him, and each time was a big disappointment. She wanted to get fucked real good at least once, so she could feel like a whole woman again. The entire time she was telling him this she was staring at him as if he were a piece of meat or something she wanted to devour.

The aunt became more and more aggressive toward him when they were alone. Once she found out that her niece was a heavy sleeper, she would press him hard to give her some attention, grinding her body against him and touching him every chance she got. She would tell him how she'd listen to him fucking her niece and wanted to get fucked just like that. She was at her sexual peak and needed some dick.

After a while, he couldn't take it anymore. One night his wife was out with her girlfriends at a club. Alone with the aunt, he gave her what she'd been asking for. She'd gone into the bathroom to take a

bath. She hated taking showers. In prison she had had no choice but to take showers, and she had promised herself that
when she got out, she would never take a shower again. She came into the living room wearing a long football jersey and sat down next to him. With a big smile on her face, she told him that she didn't have any panties on; then she showed him that she didn't have any panties on. In an instant, they were all over each other having sex like crazy. The next day he felt guilty, but that didn't stop him from having sex with her again a few nights later. She did all kinds of freaky things to him that his fiancée never did.

His fiancée got suspicious. Her aunt had been acting peculiar, always smiling and singing around the house like she was happy in love. Finally she asked him point blank if he was having sex with her aunt. He denied it, of course. How could she think such a thing? She said she was sorry and didn't want him to think she didn't trust him. But she'd caught her aunt staring at him a couple of times with a funny look in her eyes, and her mother had warned her that her sister was a little wild.

The next day he had a serious talk with the aunt and told her that they couldn't have sex anymore because her niece was getting suspicious. The aunt moved out six months later, but he dropped by her new place occasionally to visit and have sex because it was so different with her.

Convenience and proximity—the simple fact of sharing a house or apartment—and the need for sexual gratification are not the only reasons a woman will make a move on a relative's man. Jealousy and envy often provide ample motivation. A woman I knew from working at Platinum Bound Records was a model and had been in videos for rap groups we handled.

The model was sexy and knew it. She would boast that she could have any man she wanted—married or single, it didn't matter to her. She had two older sisters. One was happily married with two beautiful daughters, a wonderful house in Cherry Hill, N.J., and a nice career. She said her sister was always bragging about her wonderful, happy life. How blessed she was to have a loving, thoughtful, handsome husband with a great career; how terrific her sex life was; and how her husband couldn't get enough of her.

When she needed a place to stay until her next modeling job started in Miami, her sister said it was okay for her to stay with them. After a week of living in her sister's house, she was jealous of the life her sister had. The second week, she started walking around the house half-naked when her sister wasn't there. Sometimes she'd leave the bathroom door open so the husband could see her taking a bath. Other times, after a shower, she would walk around with just a towel wrapped around her to test his reactions.

After a while, she noticed her brother-in-law paying her more attention. He'd come into her room and ask about the videos she'd made, the different artists she'd dated, and the wild sex parties that must have taken place after shooting the videos.

Then one day he came into her room after she'd taken a shower. She dropped the towel to the floor. He had a dumb look on his face at first so she asked him if he wanted to fuck her. They had sex in her room, and it was just as good as she promised it would be. After that, they had sex every chance they could until she left for Miami.

Her sister, she said, never seemed to notice anything. The day she was packing to leave for the airport, her brother-in-law came into her room. He gave her a big hug and an envelope. She thanked him, threw the envelope into her carry-on bag, and went back to her packing.

Her sister came in a little while later to tell her how happy she was that she had come to visit. Even if it was only for a little while, her daughters had had an opportunity to get to know their aunt. The model noticed that her sister wasn't her usual outgoing, bubbly self and asked if anything was the matter. Well, yes. Her husband had been acting funny lately, she said, and she didn't understand why. They used to talk about everything and anything, but now they hardly ever touched or talked. He told her it wasn't her; that he'd been tired and burned out from all the extra work at the office. She didn't believe him and thought he was having an affair with someone at work. She didn't know what she would do if her husband left her and her baby girls for another woman.

The model sister felt like shit at that moment. She had never really thought through the consequences of her actions—how having sex with her sister's husband might affect her sister and her marriage. She told her not to worry too much; everything would be okay. Her husband might have a lot on his mind at work and not another woman in his life.

Her sister got up off the bed and hugged her tightly, telling her how much she loved her and was going to miss her. She was welcome to come stay with them anytime she wanted; her daughters were crazy about her. Then she gave her an envelope and hugged her again.

Once the model sister checked into her hotel in Miami, she opened the envelope her brother-in-law had given her. Inside were twenty hundred-dollar bills and a card that wished her good luck and knock'em dead. She had mixed feelings about the money; it made her feel like a whore.

Next she opened the envelope her sister had given her. Inside was a card, but this one read: "You are the best little sister a big sister ever had to love. Always, your big sister." There was also a traveler's check for a thousand dollars. She felt two inches tall for causing so much trouble in her sister's marriage. She prayed everything would get back to normal. She cried herself to sleep. The next day, she mailed the check back to her sister and then called her to thank her for everything.

Her sister's marriage didn't get back on track right away. Her husband began an affair with a woman from work. After he stopped seeing the other woman, the couple started going to a marriage counselor. The model sister believes that, out of spite and jealousy, she fucked up her sister's marriage. Had she not had sex with her brother-in-law, he might never have been interested in being with another woman.

These stories are only three taken from the many I've been told over the years. They spell out why you should be careful before you let a female relative move into your happy or not-so-happy home. There are many sincere, loyal female relatives and girlfriends who would never think of your man as anything but yours. But there are others who will smile in your face, but are jealous and envy the life you have.

Advice on How You Can Assess the Situation

1. First, you have to know your husband or boyfriend. Is he an honest, loyal, faithful, and loving man? Your past and present experiences will tell you whether you can trust him with a female relative around.
2. If your experiences have been good, then you have little to worry about.
3. If, however, your experiences have been mostly negative and he's working on rebuilding the trust he once had with you, you should think twice about letting a female relative or girlfriend move in with your family.
4. You should consider how well you know your female relative or girlfriend. We all have relatives or friends we've known since childhood. Once they become adults, we only see or talk to them every few months. So do you really know them as well as you think you do? People change when you're not around them as you used to be.
5. Do you have an honest and trusting relationship with the female relative or girlfriend, one built on loyalty? That is a basic requirement if she asks to move in with you until she gets on her feet or while she's in town visiting.
6. If she's betrayed a trust in the past, you need to think long and hard before letting her stay with you and your husband or boyfriend.

7. You also need to consider how long the female relative or girlfriend needs to stay. The less time, the better, especially if you have doubts about the trust level you have with either that friend or relative or with your husband or boyfriend.

If everything feels okay, then go with it. But if the situation feels uncomfortable or makes you uneasy, turn down the relative's request. It's better to say No now than have someone you love and care about tell you later that she didn't mean to hurt you or that he never meant for anything to happen. Like the black women of the past, you have to protect your home, family, and marriage or relationship by any means available. It's better to have a few hard feelings because you told a female relative or girlfriend that she couldn't stay with you than to have your marriage or relationship destroyed. At the end of the day, your marriage or relationship is what counts.

Chapter 17

A Mama's Boy

Black women, don't beat yourself up after a breakup or a divorce over what you think might have gone wrong or what you should have done to keep him in love with you. If you had a wonderful and happy marriage or relationship for two, five, ten, or perhaps thirty years, and your husband or boyfriend stops wanting to be with you, it doesn't mean he never loved you or doesn't love you anymore. It's just that people change in life and grow apart. Be thankful for the memories you made together and appreciate the love you once had.

A mother plays a crucial role in a black man's life. Sometimes the tight bond overshadows his relationship with his wife or girlfriend. A black mother, even when she acts with what she thinks are the best of intentions, can warp a son's perspective and put his wife or girlfriend on the defensive.

Most black boys are brought up to revere their mothers, to think they can do no wrong. Their mothers' opinions continue to carry a heavy weight with them when they reach adulthood

Many black women I've talked to over the years believed their marriages or long-term relationships were hurt, harmed, or even destroyed by the machinations of their partners' mothers. I could sympathize with their complaints, even their accusations, because until a few years back I was a mama's boy. I thought I was doing what every son in the black community should do—take care of his mother, look out for her, and always be there for his mama.

But sometimes the love a son holds for his mother can blind him for life. My younger brother, for example, believes our mother can do no wrong. But as black men we must realize that our wonderful, loving mothers are human too. They make mistakes just as everyone else does. They want the best for their sons, but often that is what they think is best.

One time I was seeing a lady my mother disliked. She thought she wasn't right for me and wanted me to be with someone else so she told my lady something that wasn't true. When I related the incident to my brother on the phone, he hung up on me. He didn't want to hear it. It didn't matter to him what our mother said or did. He just didn't want to hear it, period. I understood how he felt because for years my mother could do no wrong in my eyes. But then I realized my mother was human and made mistakes even when she meant nothing but the best for me.

Many black women are afraid to say anything to their husbands or boyfriends when their mothers are interfering and hurting their marriages or relationships. Often when a woman did mention to her partner the problems she was having with his mother, he would turn on her, becoming defensive and even sometimes a little ugly. To keep the peace, she would stop bringing up the slights and sly comments, even though she knew his mother's behavior was hurting her marriage or relationship.

A lot of black women, I now realize, don't know how to deal with their partners' mothers. They generally adopt one of two stances: they confront their partners or they ignore the situation entirely. There are those who do tell their husbands and boyfriends about the negative thing their mothers have done, the disparaging comments they've made, or the disrespectful treatment they've handed out. But the sons don't believe them. They cannot fathom that their sweet, loving mothers could do or say anything wrong, and they refuse to listen. Then there are those women who recognize the dangers of criticizing a mother and back off. The issue doesn't disappear; it just goes underground and never gets talked about, never resolved.

Both approaches to the mother problem come at a cost. Inevitably the marriages or relationships suffer, sometimes terminally. The women who stayed in the marriages and relationships with mama's boys weren't happy, but remained in them because of their children or because they weren't ready financially to leave.

The mama' boy I'm talking about wants to make his mother happy and proud no matter what it takes, even if it costs him the love and care of his wife or girlfriend. He pays attention to his mother's advice and follows it, convinced that she know what's best for him. He listens to his mother before he listens or talks to his wife or girlfriend. However much a son loves his mother, his wife should come first.

I used to fall hook, line, and sinker for the games my mother played. I would try to persuade my lady to agree with what my mother wanted and was blind to how siding with my mother was hurting my relationship with my lady. My mother also had a habit of talking to me or leaving messages on our answering machine as if my lady didn't exist or didn't matter. When I talked to my mother about it, she would act as if it was an accident and she didn't mean anything by it. In the beginning, I believed her, but then she repeated the performance over and over and I realized she really did act as if I was the only one who lived there.

My mother's behavior used to drive my lady crazy. She was always respectful and would bend over backwards to please my mother. All she wanted was to be accepted and respected by my mother. My mother, on the other hand, wanted to keep control and her actions were designed to undermine anyone or anything that threatened that control.

Warning Signs That He Might Be a Mama's Boy

1. He always caters to his mother's wants and needs.
2. His mother knows more about him and his feelings than you do.
3. In his eyes his mother can do or say nothing wrong.
4. He listens to whatever advice his mother gives him without talking to you first.
5. His mother goes on most of the trips or vacations you take. Even when you plan to go alone as a couple, she somehow finds a way to come along for the ride.
6. He spends more time with his mother over at her house than he does with you.
7. His mother can come and go as she pleases in your home.
8. You find yourself in an argument whenever you bring up his mother's comments or behavior toward you.
9. No matter what you try to do, you can't make his mother like you. She's always saying negative things about you.
10. Whenever you have an argument or fight, he goes over to his mother's house for the night or for a few days.

Every woman loves a man who loves and respects his mother. It shows how much he cares about women. But however much a son loves and cares for his mother, he should not let his mother run his life or control decisions that affect his marriage or relationship.

Chapter 18

Not Worth Dying For

Black men have to become better husbands and fathers. Children learn how to treat others and themselves by watching. Black boys learn how to treat black girls and then black women from the way they see the black men in their lives treating black women. Black fathers must show their sons how to respect women by example and that includes teaching them about the dangers of unprotected casual sex. The same goes for young black girls. They learn how they can expect to be treated from the way their mothers and other female relatives are treated by the men in their lives. If the young girl's mother accepts ugly treatment and abuse, that girl grows up to think that it is normal for boys and later for men to mistreat and abuse. She doesn't learn that she can just say No.

Sexually transmitted diseases (STDs) and sexually transmitted infections (STIs) have hit hardest in black communities because of the dishonesty that characterizes so many black marriages and relationships. A lot of black men have STDs or STIs, including the HIV virus, but don't know they are infected. Often they haven't been tested.

Many realize that the lifestyles they lead and have led in the past put them at risk and they should get tested. But they refuse, either because they are afraid of the results or just don't care. No black woman should take a man's word about his STD or STI status. She needs to see the actual test results.

Talking about a black man's sexual history with him can be sensitive. But that is a sensitivity black women cannot afford today. As black people, we must learn to talk to one another about our sexuality and sexual habits before we even think about that first kiss. As many have discovered, a first kiss can lead to much greater intimacy.

STDs and STIs have created a crisis in the black community. I have met a lot of angry black men out there who caught STDs or the HIV virus from a woman and want to infect other women any chance they get out of revenge.

AIDS is a deadly disease, but we must talk to our mates not only about AIDS; we have to discuss other STDs and STIs as well, now rather than later. If you haven't had this talk already with your husband or boyfriend, sit down tonight and have it. You need to know his status, given all the horrible things that can happen to him, you, and your family.

The HIV virus hits disproportionately in black communities. Blacks represent 12 percent of the U.S. population, but in 2010 accounted for 44 percent of new infections and 41 percent of the people already living with HIV infection.

Moreover, the incidence is almost twice as high for black heterosexual women as it is for black heterosexual men. AIDS is the leading cause of death among black women between the ages of twenty-five and thirty-four; it is the second leading cause of death among black men between the ages of thirty-five and forty-five.

One of the reasons is that the highest rate of infection is among men who have sex with other men (MSM). MSM represent 4 percent of the U.S. population, but 78 percent of new HIV infections. Greatest at risk are young black men and boys between the ages of thirteen and twenty-four. This group represents 55 percent of new infections overall. Many black MSM don't consider themselves homosexual and have sex regularly with unsuspecting women.

Washington, D.C. has the highest HIV/AIDs rate of any U.S. city with 3.2 percent of its residents affected, and heterosexual transmission is the leading cause of the new cases. While 52 percent of black males with AIDS were infected by other men, 77 percent of black women were infected through heterosexual contact with men on the down low, living the lie of being heterosexual when they were really bisexual or were infected while incarcerated. In 2010, the Centers for Disease Control (CDC) increased efforts to test African Americans for HIV by investing $62 million in an expanded testing program.

Although more than twenty drugs have been approved to treat HIV/AIDs, their effectiveness is limited in certain cases by two factors: The virus is mutating into drug-resistant strains, or the patients do not take their drugs as prescribed. The number of infections will probably increase as the people infected with drug- resistant strains continue to have sex or to share needles.

HIV is the most alarming of the sexually transmitted infections or viruses. But it accounts for only 50,000 new cases a year and that figure is holding steady. What is ballooning are the figures for the seven other STIs: Chlamydia, gonorrhea, hepatitis B (HBV), herpes simplex virus type 2 (HSV-2), human papilloma virus (HPV), syphilis, and trichomoniasis.

The CDC 2013 estimates peg the number of new infections overall at 20 million annually with 110 million men and women across the United States already living with STIs. Most troubling for controlling the spread of the viruses is that one in eight don't know they are infected—that's almost 13 million sexually active individuals who could be unwittingly infecting their partners.

Half of all new infections occur in men and women between the ages of fifteen and twenty-four. Four of these STIs are easily treated if diagnosed early: Chlamydia, gonorrhea, syphilis, and trichomoniasis. If undiagnosed and untreated, however, Chlamydia or gonorrhea can lead to chronic pelvic pain in women and increase the risk of ectopic pregnancies or infertility.

With the spread of STDs and STIs and its prevalence in black communities, it is imperative that you know the sexual history of the man you are letting into your bed. The choice you make might cost you your health, your ability to have children, or your life. No person can be careless in his or her sexual activity or choice of partner.

You can get an STD or STI from vaginal, oral, or anal sex. You should consult your doctor or gynecologist about methods of preventing STDs or STIs. The number-one way is abstinence; the second-best way is to use a condom for vaginal, oral, and anal sex. If a man is performing oral sex on you, he should be using a dental dam and not just his tongue. You cannot trust your health to the hands, tongue, or penis of a man you hardly know.

Black women are fifteen times more likely to be diagnosed with an STD or STI than white women. Don't be afraid to talk to the man you are dating or seeing about using condoms because you are afraid he will reject you or think you sleep around. It's a question of your health, not his feelings. If he's too good to talk about protection, then he's not worth your time or your love.

STIs and STDs have not gone away and they are not going down for black women in America. Not only do black women need to get tested; the men in their lives must be tested. Until they are, they should get no more cookies, sex, loving, or whatever you want to call it. As a black woman you need to put the brakes on the sex until you and the man have both been tested. You cannot take a man's word that he took the test and his results were negative. You need firsthand proof about what's going on with his health as well as yours.

If a man gives you attitude when you demand information on his sexual history, let him run off. He's not worth the risk. You might save yourself from contracting an STI, wrecking your health and even, in the case of HIV/AIDs, an ugly death. As Woody Allen quipped, "I'm not afraid of dying. I just don't want to be there when it happens." You certainly don't want to be there if it happens because of AIDS. There is not yet a cure for the deadly virus.

The CDC, in fact, has revised its recommendations to make HIV testing a routine part of medical care. The CDC's recommendations call for HIV screening for patients aged thirteen to sixty in all health- care settings and without the need for separate parental written consent. People at high risk should be tested annually. The recommendations emphasize the importance of voluntary testing, noting that patients can decline or opt out if they choose.

One reason for the proposed routine testing is that 250,000 Americans have HIV and are unaware they have been infected and could unwittingly be spreading the virus to their partners. The CDC estimates that new sexually transmitted cases of HIV could be reduced by more than 30 percent annually if people between the ages of thirteen and sixty-four were tested.

Half of all new STI cases each year will be among those aged fifteen to twenty-four, and blacks are at the highest risk. That statistic will continue to grow unless we educate our young black teens. Young people represent a quarter of the Americans who are having sex, but account for almost half of the new STI cases. According to the CDC, black girls and women aged fifteen to twenty- four have the highest rates of Chlamydia.

Genital human papilloma virus or HPV is the most common STI, striking at least half of all sexually active people. Low-risk strains of the virus can cause genital warts, while high-risk strains can lead to cervical cancer.

Just in case you need more reasons to practice safe sex, the CDC recently announced that gonorrhea might soon be untreatable. Currently, ceftriaxone is the only antibiotic still effective in treating gonorrhea, but it is losing its potency. Again rates of gonorrhea are highest among African Americans, sexually active teenagers, and young adults.

Before getting into a relationship or having sex with someone, you should educate yourself by googling the CDC.

Steps to Take to Protect Yourself

1. Get informed about STDs and STIs, including HIV.
2. Get tested and treated if you are positive.
3. Use protection.
4. Talk to other black women about STIs, including HIV/AIDs, and STDs.
5. Talk to your husband or boyfriend, children and family about STIs and STDs.

The best way to avoid the risk of STIs and STDs is to be tested and get married to someone infection free. You don't have to worry if you are both faithful and monogamous. But married black women still need to be aware of what's going on with their husbands, especially if they have been players. The key is whether you have a monogamous relationship.

No matter how healthy a man looks or how educated he may be, or how great his career is, it's what may be inside him that you need to be concerned about. One in five women in the United States will be infected with the herpes virus. Who do you think is giving it to them? Men.

We're getting complacent. With new medicines and diagnostics, we think STIs are manageable. The message is the same everyday and everywhere. Wear a condom when you have sex. We hear it so often we tune it out. But here's some news. Teenagers aged fourteen to seventeen are the most responsible age group in terms of using condoms (84 percent for boys and 89 percent for girls). The rates plummet after forty. Only 20 percent of women between forty and forty-nine indicate they use condoms during sex, while 36 percent of men in that age group use them.

Any black woman should buy and have her own condoms. I ran across an old friend I hadn't seen in years and was surprised to see that she was pregnant. She told me that a black man had put holes in the condom he used when he had sex with her so he would get her pregnant and he could keep her in his life. She was devastated; she knew almost nothing about this man. She later found out that the man was fifty-two although he had told her when they first met that he was forty-five. He also said he owned his business, but he actually didn't even have a job.

With all the games being played and lies being told, you can't trust yourself when it comes to your body. If he can't wait to go get tested at a health center or is too embarrassed, there is now a home HIV test, OraQuick, on the market. All you need to do is to collect a little spit from the inside of your mouth with a swab, and you'll know whether you are infected. It's the first over-the-counter home test for HIV that doesn't require users to send the test to a lab. All you have to do is place the swab, attached to a test strip, in a vial of liquid and two colored lines appear if the virus is present.

With OraQuick and the other available tests for STIs there's no excuse not to know your status or your partner's or to let yourself be pressured into having unprotect sex with someone whose sexual history you are not sure about. Don't be afraid to question the man you're dating or seeing about his sexual history.

Questions You Should Ask the Man You Are Dating or Seeing

1. Does he have other women that he's seeing sexually?
2. Did he always use protection with every woman he has had sex with? Does he still?
3. What does he want in a woman or mate?
4. Has he been tested for HIV? Other STIs? How long ago? If it's over two years, he should get tested again before starting a sexual relationship with you.
5. Is he willing to take an HIV test together before starting a sexual relationship? If he isn't, move on.
6. Has he ever engaged n any kind of sexual act with a man? Use the term "sexual act" rather than homosexual act

> because some foolish-minded black men think there's a difference.

If he's shocked or surprised you asked him questions like these, tell him he shouldn't be offended. Your concern demonstrates that you are a responsible black woman who cares about her body and anyone she lets be a part of it. He should be happy that you're willing to answer any questions he has about you and to take an HIV test with him. Older black men and women must also exercise caution as many are getting back into the dating scene after years of being married or in long-term relationships, yet only one in five women aged fifty-five to sixty-five uses condoms all the time.

You only have one life to live. It's not worth risking it for a stranger or a player for some thrills. If you're out getting your drink on or smoke on, remember that alcohol and marijuana weaken your guard. In the heat of the moment, he'll tell you he's been tested and you don't have anything to worry about. Don't fall for that weak lie. Make him wear a condom or leave.

HIV and other STIs carry a social stigma so a lot of people don't feel comfortable talking about them or getting tested, which only makes the problem worse. But before you decide you want a man in your life, before you know you can trust him with your body, you need to know about him—and that includes talking about his sexual history and habits.

Chapter 19

A Last Word and Some Resources

I've played a lot of games in the past that hurt women I loved. That's one of the reasons why I wrote this book. I wanted black women to hear, from the horse's mouth, about the games black men play on them and warn them about how dangerous or painful those games can be.

The heartbreaker, and eye-opener, came for me when a beautiful and loving black woman told me after being together for almost four years that she wished she had never met me. We were in my SUV and she started singing a Heather Headley song. *"I wish I could go back to the day before we met, so I could skip the regrets."*

The whole time she was singing, she was staring straight at me. I could feel and see all the pain I had caused this beautiful, loving woman; I could hear it in her voice. Tears were running down her cheeks. I knew she loved me, but it was no good. I was ready to love, but not ready to give up the street life.

So this book is in part expiation for past sins. But only in part. Over time I realized the great damage that players can cause and wanted to use my experiences in a positive way—to help black women avoid the traps that black men can catch them in. Driving the writing of this book is my deep hope that the thoughts of black women who read it will never echo the lines in Heather Headley's song.

There are many sources, online and toll-free numbers, where you can get information and support if you find yourself an unwilling participant in one of the games black men play on women.

Women's Health and Sexuality

Planned Parenthood (www.plannedparenthood.org) runs a nation-wide network of health centers for women. To find the health center nearest you, click on the health locator button on the website or call 1-800-230-PLAN or 1-800-230-7526. The website features special sections—Info for Teens and Tools for Parents—as well as information on women's health issues, body image, sex and sexuality, birth control, and STDs.

Domestic violence

Various sites offer online support and chat rooms for women in or recovering from abusive situations.

After Silence (www.aftersilence.org)
Message boards, chat, and shared stories for women recovering from domestic abuse and violence.

Domestic Shelters (https://www.domesticshelters.org)
The site's Facebook page has occasional professional advice as well as daily conversations for women to share opinions and unvarnished stories.

Fort Refuge (www.fortrefuge.com)
This grassroots site is smaller than some of the others, but is an active conversation place with chat rooms, forums, and a library of articles.

National Domestic Violence Hotline
1-800-799-7233 in English and Spanish

9:00 a.m. – 7:30 p.m. Central Time, Monday through Friday.

Pandora's Project (www.pandys.org)
Pandora's Aquarium, part of Pandora's Project, offers rape counseling, information, and support resources, including retreat weekends, to victims of rape and their families.

Resources for Teens

On Your Mind (www.onyourmind.net)
The site covers a broad spectrum of issues of concern to teens: depression, suicide, cutting, abusive relationships. Monday – Thursday, 4:30 p.m. – 9:30 p.m., Pacific Time (closed during summer school vacation). For any teen in immediate danger or crisis, there is a hotline available: 1-800-273-TALK (8255).

Love Is Respect: National Teen Dating Helpline
(www.loveisrepect.org)
Site focuses on ending teen dating abuse and offers real-time one-on-one support from trained peer advocates.

State Coalitions

State agencies for domestic violence and sexual assault have joined forces with local shelters, programs and agencies to form statewide coalitions to combat sexual assault and domestic violence and to give support to victims.

Alabama Coalition Against Domestic Violence
P.O. Box 4762 Montgomery,
AL 36101
(334) 832-4842 Fax: (334) 832-4803
(800) 650-6522 Hotline
Website: www.acadv.org Email:
info@acadv.org
Find Help & Statistics: Alabama

Alaska Network on Domestic and Sexual Violence
130 Seward Street, Ste 214
Juneau, AK 99801
(907) 586-3650 Fax: (907) 463-4493
Website: www.andvsa.org
Email: info@andvsa.org
Find Help & Statistics: Alaska

Arizona Coalition to End Sexual & Domestic Violence
2800 N. Central Ave., Ste. 1570
Phoenix, AZ 85004
(602) 279-2900 Fax: (602) 279-2980
(800) 782-6400 Toll Free
Website: www.acesdv.org
Email: info@acesdv.org
Find Help & Statistics: Arizona

Arkansas Coalition Against Domestic Violence
1401 West Capitol Avenue, Suite 170
Little Rock, AR 72201
(501) 907-5612 Fax: (501) 907-5618
(800) 269-4668 Nationwide
Website: www.domesticpeace.com Email: kbangert@domesticpeace.com Find Help & Statistics: Arkansas

California Partnership to End Domestic Violence
1107 9th St., Ste 910
Sacramento, CA 95812
(916) 444-7163 Fax: (916) 444-7165
Website: www.cpedv.org

Email: info@cpedv.org
Find Help & Statistics: California

Colorado Coalition Against Domestic Violence
1120 Lincoln Street, Suite 900
Denver, CO 80203
(303) 831-9632 Fax: (303) 832-7067
(888) 778-7091
Website: www.ccadv.org
Find Help & Statistics: Colorado

Connecticut Coalition Against Domestic Violence
912 Silas Deane Highway, Lower Level
Wethersfield, CT 06109
(860) 282-7899 Fax: (860) 282-7892
(888) 774-2900 In State DV Hotline
(844) 831-9200 In State DV Hotline (Spanish) Website: www.ctcadv.org
Email: contactus@ctcadv.org
Find Help & Statistics: Connecticut

Delaware Coalition Against Domestic Violence
100 West 10th Street, #703
Wilmington, DE 19801
(302) 658-2958 Fax: (302) 658-5049
(800) 701-0456 Statewide
Website: www.dcadv.org Email: dcadvadmin@dcadv.org
Find Help & Statistics: Delaware

DC Coalition Against Domestic Violence 5
Thomas Circle Northwest Washington,
DC 20005
(202) 299-1181 Fax: (202) 299-1193

Website: www.dccadv.org
Email: info@dccadv.org
Find Help & Statistics: District of Columbia
Florida Coalition Against Domestic Violence 425
Office Plaza
Tallahassee, FL 32301
(850) 425-2749 Fax: (850) 425-3091
(850) 621-4202 TDD
(800) 500-1119 In State
Website: www.fcadv.org Find
Help & Statistics: Florida

Georgia Coalition Against Domestic Violence
114 New Street, Suite B
Decatur, GA 30030
(404) 209-0280 Fax: (404) 766-3800
(800) 334-2836 Crisis Line
Website: www.gcadv.org
Email: info@gcadv.org
Find Help & Statistics: Georgia

Hawaii State Coalition Against Domestic Violence
810 Richards Street
Suite 960
Honolulu, HI 96813
(808) 832-9316 Fax: (808) 841-6028
Website: www.hscadv.org
Email: admin@hscadv.org Find
Help & Statistics: Hawaii

Idaho Coalition Against Sexual and Domestic Violence
300 Mallard Drive, Suite 130
Boise, ID 83706
(208) 384-0419 Fax: (208) 331-0687

(888) 293-6118 Nationwide
Website: www.idvsa.org Email:
thecoalition@idvsa.org Find
Help & Statistics: Idaho

Illinois Coalition Against Domestic Violence
801 South 11th Street
Springfield, IL 62703
(217) 789-2830 Fax: (217) 789-1939
(217) 242-0376 TTY
Website: www.ilcadv.org
Email: ilcadv@ilcadv.org Find
Help & Statistics: Illinois

Indiana Coalition Against Domestic Violence
1915 West 18th Street, Ste. B
Indianapolis, IN 46202
(317) 917-3685 Fax: (317) 917-3695
(800) 538-3393 In State
Website: www.icadvinc.org
Email: icadv@icadvinc.org Find
Help & Statistics: Indiana

Iowa Coalition Against Domestic Violence
515 - 28th Street, Suite 104 Des
Moines, IA 50312
(515) 244-8028 Fax: (515) 244-7417
(800) 942-0333 In State Hotline Website:
www.icadv.org
Email: admin@icadv.org Find
Help & Statistics: Iowa

Kansas Coalition Against Sexual and Domestic Violence

634 Southwest Harrison Street Topeka,
KS 66603
(785) 232-9784 Fax: (785) 266-1874
Website: www.kcsdv.org Email:
coalition@kcsdv.org Find Help &
Statistics: Kansas

Kentucky Domestic Violence Association
P.O. Box 356 Frankfort,
KY 40602
(502) 695-5382 Phone/Fax
Website: www.kdva.org Email:
kdvasac@aol.com
Find Help & Statistics: Kentucky

Louisiana Coalition Against Domestic Violence
P.O. Box 77308
Baton Rouge, LA 70879
(225) 752-1296 Fax: (225) 751-8927
Website: www.lcadv.org Email:
sheila@lcadv.org
Find Help & Statistics: Louisiana

Maine Coalition To End Domestic Violence
104 Sewall St.
Augusta, ME 04330
(207) 430-8334 Fax: (207) 430-8348
Website: www.mcedv.org
Email: info@mcedv.org
Find Help & Statistics: Maine

Maryland Network Against Domestic Violence
4601 Presidents Dr. Suite 370
Lanham, MD 20706

(301) 429-3601 Fax: (301) 429-3605
Website: www.mnadv.org
Email: info@mnadv.org
Find Help & Statistics: Maryland

Jane Doe, Inc./Massachusetts Coalition Against Sexual Assault and Domestic Violence
14 Beacon Street, Suite 507
Boston, MA 02108
(617) 248-0922 Fax: (617) 248-0902
(617) 263-2200 TTY/TDD
Website: www.janedoe.org
Email: info@janedoe.org
Find Help & Statistics: Massachusetts

Michigan Coalition Against Domestic and Sexual Violence
3893 Okemos Road, Suite B-2
Okemos, MI 48864
(517) 347-7000 Phone/TTY Fax: (517) 248-0902
Website: www.mcadsv.org Email:
general@mcadsv.org Find Help &
Statistics: Michigan

Minnesota Coalition for Battered Women
60 E. Plato Blvd., Suite 130 St.
Paul, MN 55107
(651) 646-6177 Fax: (651) 646-1527
(651) 646-0994 Crisis Line
(800) 289-6177 Nationwide
Website: www.mcbw.org
Email: mcbw@mcbw.org
Find Help & Statistics: Minnesota

Mississippi Coalition Against Domestic Violence

P.O. Box 4703 Jackson,
MS 39296
(601) 981-9196 Fax: (601) 981-2501
(800) 898-3234
Website: www.mcadv.org Email:
dvpolicy@mcadv.org
Find Help & Statistics: Mississippi

Missouri Coalition Against Domestic and Sexual Violence
718 East Capitol Avenue
Jefferson City, MO 65101
(573) 634-4161 Fax: (573) 636-3728
Website: www.mocadsv.org Email:
mocadsv@mocadsv.org Find Help &
Statistics: Missouri

Montana Coalition Against Domestic & Sexual Violence
P.O. Box 818 Helena,
MT 59624
(406) 443-7794 Fax: (406) 443-7818
(888) 404-7794 Nationwide
Website: www.mcadsv.com
Email: mcadsv@mt.net
Find Help & Statistics: Montana

Nebraska Domestic Violence Sexual Assault Coalition
1000 "O" Street, Suite 102
Lincoln, NE 68508
(402) 476-6256 Fax: (402) 476-6806
(800) 876-6238 In State Hotline
(877) 215-0167 Spanish Hotline
Website: www.ndvsac.org Email:
help@ndvsac.org
Find Help & Statistics: Nebraska

Nevada Network Against Domestic Violence
250 South Rock Boulevard, Suite 116
Reno, NV 89502
(775) 828-1115 Fax: (775) 828-9911
Website: www.nnadv.org Find
Help & Statistics: Nevada

New Hampshire Coalition Against Domestic and Sexual Violence
P.O. Box 353 Concord,
NH 03302
(603) 224-8893 Fax: (603) 228-6096
(866) 644-3574 In State
Website: www.nhcadsv.org
Email: info@nhcadsv.org
Find Help & Statistics: New Hampshire

New Jersey Coalition for Battered Women
1670 Whitehorse Hamilton Square Trenton,
NJ 08690
(609) 584-8107 Fax: (609) 584-9750
(800) 572-7233 In State
Website: www.njcbw.org
Email: info@njcbw.org
Find Help & Statistics: New Jersey

New Mexico Coalition Against Domestic Violence
201 Coal Avenue Southwest
Albuquerque, NM 87102
(505) 246-9240 Fax: (505) 246-9434
(800) 773-3645 In State
Website: www.nmcadv.org

Email: info@nmcadv.org
Find Help & Statistics: New Mexico

New York State Coalition Against Domestic Violence
350 New Scotland Avenue
Albany, NY 12054
(518) 482-5464 Fax: (518) 482-3807
(800) 942-6906 English-In State
(800) 942-6908 Spanish-In State
Website: www.nyscadv.org Email:
nyscadv@nyscadv.org Find Help &
Statistics: New York

North Carolina Coalition Against Domestic Violence
3710 University Drive, Suite 140
Durham, NC 27707
(919) 956-9124 or (888) 997-9124
Fax: (919) 682-1449
Website: www.nccadv.org
Find Help & Statistics: North Carolina

North Dakota Council on Abused Women's Services
418 East Rosser Avenue, Suite 320
Bismark, ND 58501
(701) 255-6240 Fax: (701) 255-1904
(888) 255-6240 Nationwide
Website: www.ndcaws.org
Email: ndcaws@ndcaws.org
Find Help & Statistics: North Dakota

Ohio Domestic Violence Network
4807 Evanswood Drive, Suite 201
Columbus, OH 43229
(614) 781-9651 Fax: (614) 781-9652

(614) 781-9654 TTY
(800) 934-9840
Website: www.odvn.org Email:
info@odvn.org

Action Ohio Coalition for Battered Women
5900 Roche Drive, Suite 445
Columbus, OH 43229
(614) 825-0551 Fax: (614) 825-0673
(888) 622-9315 In State
Website: www.actionohio.org Email:
actionohio@sbcglobal.net Find Help
& Statistics: Ohio

Oklahoma Coalition Against Domestic Violence and Sexual Assault
3815 North Sante Fe Avenue, Suite 124 Oklahoma
City, OK 73118
(405) 524-0700 Fax: (405) 524-0711
Website: www.ocadvsa.org
Find Help & Statistics: Oklahoma

Oregon Coalition Against Domestic and Sexual Violence
380 Southeast Spokane Street, Suite 100
Portland, OR 97202
(503) 230-1951 Fax: (503) 230-1973
(877) 230-1951
Website: www.ocadsv.com
Email: adminasst@ocadsv.com
Find Help & Statistics: Oregon

Pennsylvania Coalition Against Domestic Violence
6400 Flank Drive, Suite 1300
Harrisburg, PA 17112

(717) 545-6400 Fax: (717) 545-9456
(800) 932-4632 Nationwide
Website: www.pcadv.org
Find Help & Statistics: Pennsylvania

Puerto Rico Coalition Against Domestic Violence and Sexual Assault
Coordinadora Paz Para La Mujer
P.O. Box 193008 San
Juan, PR 00919 (787)
281-7579
Email: pazmujer@prtc.net
Find Help & Statistics: Puerto Rico

The Office of Women Advocates
Apartado 11382
San Juan, Puerto Rico 00910-1382 (787)
721-7676 Fax: (787) 725-9248

Rhode Island Coalition Against Domestic Violence
422 Post Road, Suite 202
Warwick, RI 02888
(401) 467-9940 Fax: (401) 467-9943
(800) 494-8100 In State
Website: www.ricadv.org
Email: ricadv@ricadv.org
Find Help & Statistics: Rhode Island

South Carolina Coalition Against Domestic Violence and Sexual Assault
P.O. Box 7776 Columbia,
SC 29202
(803) 256-2900 Fax: (803) 256-1030
(800) 260-9293 Nationwide

Website: www.sccadvasa.org
Find Help & Statistics: South Carolina
South Dakota Coalition Against Domestic Violence & Sexual Assault
P.O. Box 141 Pierre,
SD 57501
(605) 945-0869 Fax: (605) 945-0870
(800) 572-9196 Nationwide
Website: www.southdakotacoalition.org Email:
pierre@sdcadvsa.org
Find Help & Statistics: South Dakota

Tennessee Coalition Against Domestic and Sexual Violence
2 International Plaza Drive, Suite 425
Nashville, TN 37217
(615) 386-9406 Fax: (615) 383-2967
(800) 289-9018 In State
Website: www.tcadsv.org
Email: tcadsv@tcadsv.org
Find Help & Statistics: Tennessee

Texas Council on Family Violence
P.O. Box 161810 Austin,
TX 78716
(512) 794-1133 Fax: (512) 794-1199
Website: www.tcfv.org
Find Help & Statistics: Texas

Utah Domestic Violence Council
205 North 400 West Salt
Lake City, UT 84103
(801) 521-5544 Fax: (801) 521-5548
Website: www.udvac.org Find
Help & Statistics: Utah

Vermont Network Against Domestic Violence and Sexual Assault
P.O. Box 405 Montpelier,
VT 05601
(802) 223-1302 Fax: (802) 223-6943
(802) 223-1115 TTY
Website: www.vtnetwork.org
Email: info@vtnetwork.org Find
Help & Statistics: Vermont

Virginia Sexual & Domestic Violence Action Alliance
5008 Monument Avenue, Suite A
Richmond, VA 23230
Office: 804.377.0335 Fax: 804.377.0339
Website: www.vsdvalliance.org
Email: info@vsdvalliance.org Find
Help & Statistics: Virginia

Washington State Coalition Against Domestic Violence
711 Capitol Way, Suite Suite 702
Olympia, WA 98501
(360) 586-1022 Fax: (360) 586-1024
(360) 586-1029 TTY
1402 Third Avenue, Suite 406
Seattle, WA 98101
(206) 389-2515 Fax: (206) 389-2520
(800) 886-2880 In State
(206) 389-2900 TTY
Website: www.wscadv.org
Email: wscadv@wscadv.org
Find Help & Statistics: Washington

Washington State Native American Coalition Against Domestic and Sexual Assault
P.O. Box 13260
Olympia, WA 98508
(360) 352-3120 Fax: (360) 357-3858
(888) 352-3120
Website: www.womenspiritcoalition.org

West Virginia Coalition Against Domestic Violence
5004 Elk River Road South
Elkview, WV 25071
(304) 965-3552 Fax: (304) 965-3572
Website: www.wvcadv.org
Find Help & Statistics: West Virginia

Wisconsin Coalition Against Domestic Violence
307 South Paterson Street, Suite 1
Madison, WI 53703
(608) 255-0539 Fax: (608) 255-3560
Website: www.wcadv.org
Email: wcadv@wcadv.org
Find Help & Statistics: Wisconsin

Wyoming Coalition Against Domestic Violence and Sexual Assault
P.O. Box 236
409 South Fourth Street
Laramie, WY 82073
(307) 755-5481 Fax: (307) 755-5482
(800) 990-3877 Nationwide Website:
www.wyomingdvsa.org
Email: info@mail.wyomingdvsa.org
Find Help & Statistics: Wyoming

Legal Assistance

Women's Law (www.womenslaw.org) is the largest online chat community for sexual assault and domestic violence as well as other legal hotpoints for women.

HIV/AIDs and STD Information

National STD & Aids Hotline
1-800-342-2437

www.knowhiv/aids.org
1-866-344-KNOW(1-866-344-5669)

www.HIVtest.org to find free, fast, and confidential testing near you

Condoms

iCondom—a free iPhone app, developed in part by MTV's Staying Alive Foundation, features a user-generated maps of retailers, including stores that are open 24/7 and dispensers that are empty.

About the Author

Kareem Rice was born and raised in Philadelphia, Pennsylvania. His exposure to the games black men play started early; his father was a hard-core player. Later, as studio manager at Platinum Bound Records, subsequently Team PB, and as a security professional, he had a ring-side seat to observe players in action and the many stratagems they use to con unsuspecting black women attracted to the glamour of the music world or the excitement of the club scene.

The author can be reached by email at his website—www.kopublishing.com—and welcomes any comments or questions from readers. Books can also be ordered through the site.

Made in the USA
Middletown, DE
31 March 2022